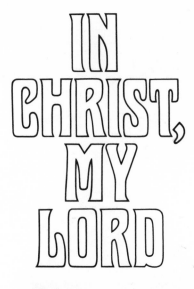

IN CHRIST, MY LORD

100 Devotional Thoughts from Luther

Barbara Owen Webb

Concordia
Publishing House
St. Louis

Copyright © 1982 Concordia Publishing House
3558 South Jefferson Avenue, St. Louis, MO 63118

Manufactured in the United States of America

Taken from the first 29 volumes of Luther's Works, American Edition, copyright © 1955—1976 Concordia Publishing House

---

Library of Congress Cataloging in Publication Data

Luther, Martin, 1483-1546.
    In Christ, my Lord.

    1. Meditations. I. Webb, Barbara Owen. II. Title.
BR331.E6E5   1982   242   81-22129
ISBN 0-570-03852-9 (pbk.)   AACR2

---

1 2 3 4 5 6 7 8 9 10 WP 91 90 89 88 87 86 85 84 83 82

Contents

Preface 7

Acknowledgments 8

Hope, *Genesis 3:15* 9

Life, *Genesis 3:20* 10

Perseverance, *Genesis 8:1* 11

Comfort, *Genesis 9:12-13* 12

A Servant, *Genesis 13:5, 7, 8a* 13

God's Benevolence, *Genesis 15:5* 14

Faith That Justifies, *Genesis 15:6* 15

A God of Seeing, *Genesis 16:13* 16

Saintly Joy, *Genesis 17:17* 17

Patient Praying, *Genesis 17:19* 18

It Is God You Hear, *Genesis 17:22* 19

God Governs His Saints, *Genesis 39:21* 20

The Sustaining Word, *Genesis 39:23* 21

Mistrust, *Deuteronomy 1:27* 22

God's Word in the Heart, *Deuteronomy 6:6* 23

I Am the Lord Your God, *Deuteronomy 8:3* 24

Festivals, *Deuteronomy 16:8* 25

A Prophet to Come, *Deuteronomy 18:15* 26

Law—Gospel, *Deuteronomy 18:15b* 27

Free for Others, *Psalm 1:3* 28

Empty Before the Lord, *Psalm 4:1* 29

The Shadow of Thy Wings, *Psalm 17:8b* 30

Hear, *Psalm 23:1* 31

My Instruction, *Psalm 32:8* 32

Christ's Lips, *Psalm 45:2* 33

His Bride and Queen, *Psalm 45:9b* 35

God of the Promise, *Psalm 51:1* 36

The Sacrifice of Righteousness, *Psalm 51:19* 37

Pour Out Your Heart, *Psalm 62:8* 38

Christ's Enemies, *Psalm 110:1* 39

Remembering Christ, *Psalm 111:4* 40

Light Rises for the Upright, *Psalm 112:4* 41

Study the Word, *Psalm 117*   42
He Is Good, *Psalm 118:1*   43
Distress, *Psalm 118:5*   44
The Holy Christian Church, *Psalm 118:20*   45
God's Righteousness, *Psalm 143:11-12*   46
My Victory, *Isaiah 12:2*   47
Hide a Little While, *Isaiah 26:20*   48
Wait, Wait, Wait, *Isaiah 30:15*   49
The Cross for Weak Hands, *Isaiah 35:3*   51
Christ Does Not Weary, *Isaiah 40:28*   52
His Understanding, *Isaiah 40:28c*   53
Faint, *Isaiah 40:29*   54
Soft-Spoken Christ, *Isaiah 42:2*   55
Forsaken for a Moment, *Isaiah 54:7*   56
Anointed to Bring Good Tidings, *Isaiah 61:1*   57
Thanksgiving, *Isaiah 61:3c*   58
All His Benefits, *Isaiah 63:7*   59
He Is Answering, *Isaiah 65:24*   60
Readiness to Forgive, *Micah 7:5*   61
Christ's Words, *Matthew 5:2-3*   62
Spiritually Poor, *Matthew 5:3a*   63
Mourning, *Matthew 5:4*   64
Works That Shine, *Matthew 5:16*   65
Forgiving Others, *Matthew 6:14-15*   66
Do So for Others, *Matthew 7:12*   67
The Magnificat, *Luke 1:46*   68
Rejoice in God, *Luke 1:47*   70
God's Regard, *Luke 1:48*   71
Resurrection, *John 6:54b*   72
Hear Him, *John 7:17*   73
Consolation, *John 14:1a*   74
Finding God, *John 14:1b*   75
Comforter, *John 14:16*   76
Peace, *John 14:27*   77
The Vinedresser, *John 15:1-2*   78
Abide in Me, *John 15:7a*   79
The Christian Estate, *John 15:7b*   81

Love One Another, *John 15:12, 14*   82
Knowing God, *John 15:15*   83
True Righteousness, *John 16:8, 10*   84
The Spirit of Truth, *John 16:13a*   85
The Speaker, the Word, and the Listener, *John 16:13c*   86
Magnifying God's Grace, *Romans 3:8*   87
Satan's Tricks, *Romans 3:27*   88
Righteousness and Peace, *Romans 5:1*   89
Love from Faith, *Romans 7:6*   90
"Feet" for the Gospel, *Romans 10:15*   91
The Work of Prayer, *Romans 12:12*   92
Bring Peace, *Romans 14:18*   93
Joy and Peace, *Romans 15:13*   94
Christ in Me, *Galatians 2:20a, b*   95
"ME", *Galatians 2:20c*   96
Inner Assurance, *Galatians 4:6*   97
Abba, *Galatians 4:6c*   98
An Heir, *Galatians 4:7b*   99
Faith—Internal and External, *Galatians 5:6*   100
Christ—Gift and Example, *Galatians 5:7-8*   101
Love Your Neighbor, *Galatians 5:14*   102
Flesh and Spirit, *Galatians 5:17*   103
His Word in the Heart, *Colossians 3:16*   104
Christ's Loving-Kindness, *Titus 3:4*   105
Christ's Humanity, *Hebrews 1:2*   106
Works Flow from Faith, *Hebrews 2:3*   107
A Pleasing Spectacle, *Hebrews 2:10*   108
Faith Through Hearing, *Hebrews 3:7*   109
Illumined from Above, *Hebrews 6:13a*   110
Loving Others, *Hebrews 10:24*   111
A Gift for Others, *Revelation 3:17*   112

Preface

One day, 16 years ago, I came to my pastor's office, feeling glum and miserable. I was weary and ashamed of my own impatience, anger, and unthoughtfulness at home, in the family. My pastor smiled sympathetically. "What you need is a good dose of Luther," he said, reaching for a large volume. I don't remember now what book it was. There have been many more since then: Luther's Commentary on Romans, on Galatians, his Large Catechism, sermons from John, lectures on Genesis, and more. But with Martin Luther's vigorous and positive words came new assurance that my sins were forgiven for Christ's sake. I was whole, loved, free to be a servant.

As I read Luther, I would sometimes get bogged down in his wordiness. Yet more often I'd catch my breath, saying, "Oh, I never thought of that" about some delightful, restoring insight. Sometimes, because I was reading a borrowed book, I'd excerpt a paragraph or two to have ready for another day when I needed "a dose of Luther."

That is how this book came about. The excerpts are little flashes of insight on a word or phrase of Scripture. Because Luther wrote extensively and sometimes redundantly with the tendency to go off on tangents, some of the excerpts have been abridged to delete excess material. Many have been reworked for easier reading by dividing Luther's very long sentences and paragraphs. Occasionally some paraphrasing has been necessary to make the excerpt clear in itself. However, great care has been taken not to change Luther's meaning but simply to restructure the commentary materials so that they have the flow of meditations.

For Luther the Good News of forgiveness because of God's work in Jesus Christ is found from Genesis to Revelation. It is the healing "medicine" that a Christian needs every day. It is hoped that the samples of Luther here may encourage you to dig further into his work.

B. O. W.

Acknowledgments

I am deeply grateful to my pastor, the Reverend G. Holmes Mendelman, for introducing me to Luther and giving me free access to his personal set of *Luther's Works* and other volumes. I thank him for his continuing and unfailing support, direction, and encouragement.

I also acknowledge with appreciation the confidence and enthusiasm given to me by the Reverend Frederick W. Kemper in support of my work on this project.

Hope

I shall put enmity between you and the woman and your seed and her seed. Genesis 3:15

These words deal specifically with the judgment of Satan. Here we find sound comfort, for these words are not spoken by God for the devil's sake. They are spoken for the sake of Adam and Eve, that, hearing this judgment, they may be comforted, realizing that God is the enemy of that being which inflicted so severe a wound on man.

Here grace and mercy begin to shine forth from the midst of the wrath which sin and disobedience aroused. Here, in the midst of most serious threats, the Father reveals His heart. This is not a father who is so angry that he would turn out his son because of his sin, but one who points to a deliverance. Indeed, this father promises victory against the enemy that deceived and conquered human nature.

Adam and Eve do not hear themselves cursed like the serpent. No, they hear themselves drawn up, as it were, in the battle line against their condemned enemy, with the hope of help from the Son of God, the Seed of the woman. Forgiveness of sins and full reception into grace are here pointed out to Adam and Eve.

Their consolation against sin and despair was their hope for this crushing of Satan by the Seed. It would be brought about in the future through Christ. And through the hope based on this promise, Adam and Eve will also rise up to eternal life on the Last Day.

LW, 1, pp. 188-191

Life

Adam called the name of his wife Eve, because she was the mother of all the living. Genesis 3:20

The name which Adam gives his wife is very pleasing and delightful. For what is more precious, better, or more delightful than life? This is the reason he gave: "Because she is the mother of all the living." It is clear from this passage that after Adam had received the Holy Spirit, he had become marvelously enlightened. He believed and understood the saying concerning the woman's Seed, who would crush the head of the serpent.

He gave an outward indication of this faith by means of his wife's name. By this designation of his wife he gave support to the hope in the future Seed. He strengthened his own faith and comforted himself with the thought that he believed in life even when all nature had already been made subject to death.

If Adam had not been aware of the future life, he would not have been able to cheer his heart, nor would he have assigned so pleasing a name to his wife. But here he gives clear indication that the Holy Spirit had cheered his heart through his trust in the forgiveness of sins by the Seed of Eve. He calls her Eve to remind himself of the promise through which he himself also received new life, and to pass on the hope of eternal life to his descendants.

This hope and faith he writes on his wife's forehead by means of the name Eve.

LW, 1, pp. 219-220

Perseverance

God remembered Noah and all the beasts and all the cattle that were with him in the ark. Genesis 8:1

It is not idle chatter when the Holy Spirit says that God remembered Noah. It indicates that from the day when Noah entered the ark nothing was said to him, nothing was revealed to him, and he saw no ray of grace shining. He clung only to the promise he had received.

Meanwhile the waters and the waves were raging as though God had surely forgotten him. His children, the cattle, and the other animals experienced the same peril throughout the entire hundred and fifty days in the ark. Even though the holy seed overcame these perils, through a rich measure of the Spirit, it did not overcome them without tears and great fear.

It was no joke or laughing matter for them to live shut up in the ark for so long, to see the endless masses of rain, to be tossed about by the waves, and to drift. In these circumstances there was the feeling that God had forgotten them. All their circumstances compelled them to debate whether God was favorably inclined and wanted to remember them. Therefore, although they overcame these hardships, they did not overcome them without awful affliction.

Let us, then, remember that this story sets before us an example of faith, perseverance, and patience, in order that those who have the divine promise may not only learn to believe it but may also realize that they need perseverance. In the New Testament Christ calls on us to persevere when He says: "He who endures to the end will be saved" (Matt. 24:13).

LW, 2, pp. 103-105

Comfort

God said: This is the sign of the covenant which I make between Me and you and every living creature that is with you, for all future generations. I set My bow in the cloud, and it shall be a sign of the covenant between Me and the earth. Genesis 9:12-13

Careful note must be taken of the phrase "for all future generations," for it includes not only the human beings of that time and the animals of that time but all their offspring until the end of the world. Furthermore, this passage also teaches us how God often links His promise with a sign, and the particular nature of signs is that they dispense comfort.

Noah and his people were in great need of such comfort. A man who has been humbled by God is unable to forget his hurt and pain. It is for this reason that God shows Himself benevolent in such a variety of ways and takes such extraordinary delight in pouring forth compassion.

This comfort is expressed in many eloquent words and emphasized by the sign of the bow to meet the need of these wretched people who had been watching the immeasurable wrath of God rage for an entire year. They could not be talked out of their fear and terror by a word or two. A great abundance of words was needed to drive back their tears and to soften their grief. Even though they were saints, they were still flesh, just as we are.

When the same promise is repeated so many times (Genesis 9:11-16), this is an indication of God's extraordinary affection for mankind. He is trying to persuade them not to fear such a punishment in the future but to hope for blessing and for the utmost forbearance.

LW, 2, pp. 144-146

A Servant

Lot, who went with Abram, also had flocks and herds . . . and there was strife between the herdsmen of Abram's cattle and the herdsmen of Lot's cattle. . . . Then Abram said to Lot: Let there be no strife. Genesis 13:5, 7, 8a

It was no minor matter that in the midst of strange nations Abram was compelled to separate from a very faithful companion and dear nephew. A faithful friend is a great boon and a precious treasure in any situation of life. He can give aid and comfort in facing common dangers and also during spiritual trials. Even if one's heart is well grounded by the Holy Spirit, it is a great advantage to have a brother with whom one can talk about religion and from whom one can hear words of comfort.

To keep us from supposing that this parting of relatives occurred as the result of insignificant events, Scripture gives weighty reasons why Abram and Lot separated. Nothing sadder could happen to Abram, yet he yields to necessity in order to avoid even greater unpleasantness.

But let us take note of the law of love and of unity. Abram was Lot's uncle; he was older; he had greater prestige because of the promise. In addition, he was a priest and prophet of the Lord. And yet, disregarding all this, he yields his right and puts himself on the same level with his nephew. "If you take the left hand," Abram says to Lot, "then I will go to the right; or if you take the right hand, then I will go to the left." He gives Lot the choice. Is this not what Christ commands in John 13:15 ff., that he who is the greater should be as the lesser and as the servant of the others?

LW, 2, pp. 335-337

God's Benevolence

God brought Abraham outside and said: Look toward heaven, and number the stars, if you are able to number them. Then He said to him: so shall your descendants be. Genesis 15:5

The fact that Abraham is commanded to look at the stars is proof that this vision occurred at night, at a time when Abraham was sighing and lamenting. It is characteristics of sublime trials to occupy hearts when they are alone. For this reason there is frequent mention in the Holy Scripture of praying at night and in solitude. Affliction is the teacher of such praying.

Thus because Abraham was occupied with these sad thoughts, he was unable to sleep. Therefore he got up and prayed; but while he is praying and feeling such great agitation within himself, God appears to him and converses with him in a friendly manner, so that Abraham, who is awake, is completely enraptured.

The trial which tormented this saintly man was not a light one. Therefore God's message to Abraham is so profuse and His encouragement so lavish, even adding a sign. Abraham is led out. He is told to look toward heaven and to count the stars. And innumerable descendants are promised him by God, who does not indulge in empty talk.

God speaks with Abraham in a manner that is no different from the way a friend speaks with a close acquaintance. It is God's practice to do so, and this is His nature.

After He has properly afflicted His own, He shows Himself most benevolent and pours Himself out completely.

LW, 3, pp. 17-18

Fa   s

Abraham believed the Lord; and he reckoned it to him as righteousness.
Genesis 15:6

Faith had previously been called for in other Genesis passages—for example, the passage about the Seed of the woman, the command to build the ark, the threat of the Flood, and the command to Abraham to leave his country. But these passages merely demand faith; they do not praise or recommend it. They do not commend faith as the verse before us does. Therefore this is one of the foremost passages of all Scripture.

If you should ask whether Abraham was righteous before this time, my answer is: He was righteous because he believed God. But here the Holy Spirit wanted to attest this expressly, since the promise deals with a spiritual Seed. He did so in order that you might conclude on the basis of a correct inference that those who accept this Seed, or those who believe in Christ, are righteous.

Abraham's faith was extraordinary, since he left his country when commanded to do so and became an exile; but we are not all commanded to do the same thing. In that earlier connection Moses does not add: "Abraham believed God, and this was reckoned to him as righteousness." But in the passage before us he makes this addition when he is speaking about the heavenly Seed. He does so in order to comfort the church of all times. He is saying that those who, with Abraham, believe this promise are truly righteous.

LW, 3, pp. 18-20

A God of Seeing

Hagar called the name of the Lord who spoke to her: Thou art a God of seeing; for she said: Have I really seen God and remained alive after seeing Him? Genesis 16:13

The Word of God is never without fruit. Therefore the rebellious, proud, and disobedient Hagar is changed when the angel speaks. She returns to her mistress and patiently submits to her authority. Not only this; she acknowledges God's mercy, praises God, and calls upon Him by a new name in order to proclaim abroad the kindness through which He had manifested Himself to her.

This example is profitable for giving us instruction in order that everyone may come to know the kindnesses of God in his vocation, may be thankful for them and proclaim them. Likewise, that we may bear with patience the chastisements inflicted by our superiors, because God takes pleasure in such patience and sends help.

It is a sacrifice of thanksgiving and a service most pleasing to God if you acknowledge and proclaim His acts of kindness and call Him "He who sees me," as if you were saying: "I thought I had been completely forsaken by God. But now I see that He had regard for me and did not cast me aside when I was in trouble."

This is a most beautiful name for God. Would that we all could bestow it on Him. We would conclude with certainty that He has regard for us and cares for us, especially when He seems to have forgotten us. For he who can say in affliction: "God sees me" has true faith and can do and bear everything, yes, he overcomes all things and is triumphant.

LW, 3, pp. 69-70

Saintly Joy

Abraham fell on his face and laughed, and said to himself: Shall a child be born to a man who is a hundred years old? Shall Sarah, who is ninety years old, bear a child? Genesis 17:17

Even though Abraham had no doubts about the promise, yet so far he was mistaken with respect to the person. For he thought that Sarah would not bear a child and that the promise would be diverted to Ishmael. But here a perfect circle is closed, so to speak, and Abraham sees that a true heir will be born to him from Sarah. Consequently, he is full of joy. Exulting and triumphing in the most beautiful and perfect faith, he falls to the ground and laughs. Full of wonderment, he says: "Shall a son be born to me, a man one hundred years old, and from Sarah at that?"

Thus Abraham, full of joy, laughs as he gives thanks to God for His so unexpected kindness. For what else could he do than marvel at this and rejoice over it?

When we read such accounts, we should justly be ashamed that a like fervor of the spirit is not felt in our hearts. Although we have the Word of God in such richness, our hearts are nevertheless harder than an anvil and, like rocky soil, keep the root of the Word without sap and fruit, while the saintly patriarchs marveled at this inexpressible benevolence of God to the point of being overcome.

Let us ask God to give us a joyful heart for such joyful promises that we, too, may exult and be glad with saintly Abraham because we are the people of God.

LW, 3, pp.153-155

Patient Praying

God said: No, but Sarah your wife shall bear you a son, and you shall call his name Isaac. I will establish My covenant with him as an everlasting covenant for his descendants after him. Genesis 17:19

One may observe here that God always grants more than we are able to ask for or to understand. Accordingly, one should learn that those who want to pray properly should accustom themselves to pray with confidence and not to be deterred either by the greatness of the things to be granted or by the unworthiness of their praying.

There is a very beautiful example in Monica, the mother of Augustine, who prayed for her son and asked for nothing else than that he be delivered from the foolish ideas of the Manichaeans and be baptized. Like an anxious mother, she also considered betrothing a girl to him if in this way he might be converted.

But the more she prayed, the more unyielding and stubborn her son became. But when the time had come for the anxious prayer to be heard (for God has a way of delaying His help), Augustine is not only converted and baptized. He devotes himself completely to the study of theology and becomes a teacher who shines in the church up to this day and teaches and instructs it.

Monica had never asked for this. She would have been satisfied to have her son delivered from his error and become a Christian. But God wants to give greater things than we are able to ask for, provided that we do not tire of praying.

LW, 3, pp. 157-160

It Is God You Hear

When He had finished talking with him, God went up from Abraham.
Genesis 17:22

It is indeed something very great to have God conversing and associating with us. Even though God does not appear to us in an extraordinary form as He did to Abraham, yet His usual and most friendly and most intimate appearance is this, that He presents Himself to us in the Word, in the use of the Keys, in Baptism, and in the Lord's Supper.

These facts must be impressed rather frequently, and it is not without reason that I am repeating them. If Abraham should be compared with us who live in the New Testament, he is, for the most part, less important than we are, provided that one considers the matter impartially. To be sure, in his case the personal gifts are greater; but God did not manifest Himself to him in a closer and more friendly manner than He does to us. Let it indeed be a great glory to have those appearances, but what greater or better advantage did Abraham have from them than the fact that God spoke with him?

This happens to us too, and indeed daily, as often as and wherever we wish. It is true that you hear a human being when you are baptized and when you partake of the Holy Supper. But the Word which you hear is not that of a human being; it is the Word of the living God. It is He who baptizes you. It is He who absolves you from sins. It is He who commands you to hope in His mercy.

LW, 3, pp. 164-166

God Governs His Saints

The Lord was with Joseph and showed him steadfast love, and gave him favor in the sight of the keeper of the prison. Genesis 39:21

Let us learn the rule and order which God is wont to employ in governing His saints. For I, too, have often attempted to prescribe to God definite methods He should use in the administration of the church or of other matters. "Ah, Lord," I have said, "I would like this to be done in this order, with this result!" But God would do the very opposite of what I had sought.

Then the thought would come to me: "Nevertheless, my plan is not disadvantageous to the glory of God. It will contribute very much toward the hallowing of Thy name, the gathering and increasing of Thy kingdom, and the propagation of the knowledge of Thy Word. It is a very fine plan and excellently thought out." But the Lord undoubtedly laughed at this wisdom and said: "Come now, I know that you are a wise and learned man; but it has never been My custom for Peter, Dr. Martin, or anyone else to teach, direct, govern, and lead Me. I am not a passive God. No, I am an active God who is accustomed to doing the leading, ruling, and directing."

Therefore, let us learn from the example of Joseph concerning the way God governs His saints. Here one sees how God carved out and formed this dearly beloved and most precious gem through great trials that were not Joseph's plans but God's plans. These things are set before the church of God and the consciences of the godly to the end that they may learn to understand the nature of the counsels and works of God.

LW, 7, pp. 100, 103-104

The Sustaining Word

The keeper of the prison paid no heed to anything that was in Joseph's care, because the Lord was with him; and whatever he did, the Lord made it prosper. Genesis 39:23

If Joseph had said: "Lord God, allow me to live with my father in Hebron," or if he had murmured against God because of the unjust accusation and captivity, and God had satisfied his wishes not to be consigned to slavery or hurled into bonds, then, according to the wisdom of his own reason, which finds it difficult to render this obedience to God, he would never have been raised to such a position of honor. But since he was full of the Holy Spirit, he submitted patiently to the Lord's will until at length he was exalted not only for his own consolation and glory but also for the temporal and spiritual welfare of Egypt. For he saw God's back and waited until God should reveal and show forth His salvation, which is far richer and far more magnificent than he would ever have had the courage to pray or hope for.

Joseph believes in the Lord, whom he does not see. He hopes to have His grace, which he does not perceive. He feels that everything unfavorable is being put in his way. Nevertheless, he receives what he has believed and hoped for.

Up to now he has walked like a blind man in the thickest darkness. He has seen neither God nor his father nor anything else than death and destruction. But he has clung to the Word which he had heard from his father: "I am the Lord your God, and the God of your fathers." This Word has been his life, and from this life he will later be raised to immeasurable glory and honor.

LW, 7, pp. 100, 105-106

Mistrust

The Lord hated us. Deuteronomy 1:27

See what a great disaster that tiny first beginning of doubt and the turning to trust in human prudence finally brings with it. Having now totally forgotten all the promises and wonders of God and being absorbed only in their own plans, the Children of Israel became worthy of listening to false messengers and preachers. Those messengers proclaim, and these people believe, greater things than the facts warrant. Instead of giving assent to the true Word of God, they give in to the lies of men.

Unbelief runs riot because the Word of God is lost, and in vain do Joshua and Caleb try to impress upon them the promise and truth of God. Godlessness conquers, and the lie wins out; truth lies prostrate. This is the fruit of human prudence and power in matters that belong to God. Finally they come to blasphemy. "The Lord hates us," they say.

This is the gratitude for the many miracles shown them. How could one ever overstate this most evil example of unbelief? After a man has begun to mistrust God, whom he previously considered propitious, he makes God an object of his hatred. For when His Word is changed, He Himself is changed; for He Himself is in His Word.

Note, therefore, that godlessness makes dangers more and greater than they are, but it cares nothing for the Word of God. On the other hand, godliness regards all dangers, even the greatest, as nothing and the Word of God as the power of God (Rom. 1:16).

LW, 9, p. 22

God's Word in the Heart

These words shall be upon your heart. Deuteronomy 6:6

Not only in a book, not only in thought, he says, but in the inmost feeling should these words be the most precious treasure. For where your treasure is, there will your heart be also (Matt. 6:21). Therefore let nothing reign in your heart except faith and the love of God. On these let your heart meditate day and night (Ps. 1:2).

For where they have first been in the heart in this way, there it will follow happily that they are also in your mouth. "And impress them on your sons"; that is, repeat and ingrain these words of faith daily, lest they become pale and cold, and grow old with rust.

Then it will follow that you will speak of them everywhere and always. Finally, bind them as a memorial on your hands and before your eyes; last of all, write them on the doorposts.

See the order of treating the Word of God: first, it is to be pondered in the heart; secondly, impressed faithfully and constantly on children by word of mouth; thirdly, discussed openly and everywhere; fourthly, written on the hand and drawn before the eyes—that is, fulfilling them in deed and pondering them; fifth and last, inscribed, and that on posts and doorways, not in books, since Moses himself has already written them in a book. He simply wants these words to meet us everywhere and to be in our memories.

LW, 9, p. 69

I Am the Lord Your God

He humbled you and fed you with manna, that He might make you know that man does not live by bread alone. Deuteronomy 8:3

To understand these and similar wonderful and faithful promises of God is truly to understand the promise of the First Commandment, in which He says: "I am the Lord your God."

"Yours, yours," He says, "who will show and display Myself to you as God and will not forsake you, if only you believe this."

This is what Moses treats in this chapter as in the midst of abundance he sets up and presents the example of manna, which was given in the midst of want, in order to call the people back from the belly to the Word. Therefore he also repeats at the conclusion: "He brought streams forth for you from hard rock and fed you with manna in the desert. . . ." For what would you less expect from a rock than water and drink? What less in the desert than bread and food? Why did He not give water from some green tree or cloud of the sky? Why not food from branches or roots or herbs?

He did this that the immeasurable care of God for us might be praised. He is willing and able to turn a rock into your drink, a desert into your food, nakedness into beautiful clothing, poverty into wealth, death into life, shame into glory, evil into good, enemies into friends. See, therefore, how fittingly and aptly Moses uses this miracle of God to explain the meaning of the First Commandment.

LW, 9, pp. 92, 94-96

Festivals

On the seventh day there shall be an assembly to the Lord your God.
Deuteronomy 16:8

Human nature tends unceasingly to set up ceremonies and institute forms for worshiping God. Therefore it is necessary that it be curbed and kept in the Word of God, through which we are sure that what we do is divinely instituted and pleases God. The Old Testament festivals also assure that the people come together at least two or three times a year, hear and learn the Law of God, and be kept in the unity of faith and life.

There are, however, three things that Moses wanted remembered at these three festivals. In the Festival of Passover the people should recall the Exodus from Egypt. At the Pentecost Festival they should remember receiving the Law on Mt. Sinai. At the Feast of Tabernacles they were to remember all the physical benefits shown in those forty years in the desert. So you see that the festivals are established for the sake of our salvation and the glory of God, that the Word of God may be heard and His blessings remembered, that we may be instructed, nourished, and preserved in faith and love.

All these festivals we celebrate by an allegory of the Spirit in one festival. For we observe the Passover every day when we proclaim and believe that Christ, the Lamb of God was offered up for us. So daily we have Pentecost when we receive the new Law, the Spirit, into our hearts (Jer. 31:33) through the ministry of the Word. Daily we celebrate the Feast of Tabernacles when we teach and experience that we are strangers in this world and sojourn in the tabernacles of our bodies which last but a short time.

LW, 9, pp. 155-157

A Prophet to Come

The Lord your God will raise up for you a Prophet like me from among you, from your brethren—Him you shall heed. Deuteronomy 18:15

This is the chief passage in this whole book and a clearly expressed prophecy of Christ as the new Teacher. Appropriately, Moses places it here at the end, after he has finished his discourses concerning the priesthood, the kingdom, the government, and the whole worship of God. It is his purpose to show that in the future there will be another priesthood, another kingdom, another worship of God, and another word, by which all of Moses will be set aside. Here Moses clearly describes his own end, and he yields his mastery to the Prophet who is to come. When Moses says: "Heed Him who will be raised up like me," he teaches plainly that his own word is different from the Word of that Prophet.

But there cannot be another word beyond the word of Moses, unless it is the Gospel, since everything that belongs to the teaching of the Law has been transmitted most perfectly and amply by Moses. For what could be added to the Decalog, to say nothing of the rest? What loftier thing can be taught then to believe, trust, love, and fear God with one's whole heart, not to tempt God, etc.? Furthermore, what rules can be more just and holy than those which Moses ordains concerning the external worship of God, government, and love of one's neighbor?

Since there cannot be another word beyond the perfect teaching of the Law unless it were the Word of grace, it follows that this Prophet will not be a teacher of the Law but a minister of grace.

LW, 9, pp. 176-177

Law—Gospel

Him you shall heed. Deuteronomy 18:15b

Unless that new Prophet were to bring another word, Moses would not need to compare Him to himself when he says: "The Lord will raise Him up, like me." All the other prophets who taught Moses were not like Moses or similar to Moses but inferior to Moses, teaching what Moses had commanded. Therefore in all of them the people did not hear anyone else but Moses himself and his words. For Moses speaks in them; they are his mouth to the people. This Prophet, however, Moses dare not subordinate to himself and put his words into His mouth. He places Him above all prophets who taught on the basis of Moses. Unless He were greater than Moses, Moses would not yield obedience and authority to Him. Moreover, unless He taught greater things, He could not be greater.

Here we have those two ministries of the Word which are necessary for the salvation of the human race: the ministry of the Law and the ministry of the Gospel. The ministry of Moses is temporary, finally to be ended by the coming of the ministry of Christ, as he says here, "Heed Him." But the ministry of Christ will be ended by nothing else, since it brings eternal righteousness and "puts an end to sin," as it is said in Dan. 9:24.

The sin and wrath which Moses arouses through his ministry that Prophet cancels through righteousness and grace by His ministry. This Prophet, therefore, demands nothing; but He grants what Moses demands.

LW, 9, pp. 176-178

Free for Others

He is like a tree planted by streams of water, that yields its fruit in its season. Psalm 1:3

To bring forth fruit indicates that this blessed man, through love, serves not himself but his neighbors. He is compared to a tree that bears fruit not for itself, but for others. In fact, no creature lives for himself or serves only himself except man and the devil. The sun does not shine for itself, water does not flow for itself. Certainly every creature serves the law of love, and its whole substance is in the Law of the Lord. Even the members of the human body do not serve only themselves. Only the passions of the heart are ungodly. For this ungodly passion not only gives no one his own, serves no one, is kind to no one, but snatches everything for itself, looks for its own in everything, even in God Himself. But this blessed man possesses the kindness of the good trees, which do no man evil but help all men, while willingly giving their fruits.

The man gives these fruits "in his season." Oh, this is a golden and lovable word, through which the freedom of the righteous Christian is affirmed! The ungodly have fixed days, fixed times, certain works, and certain places to which they are so firmly bound that even if their neighbor were to die of starvation, they could not tear themselves away to help. But that blessed man is free at all times, in every work, for every place, and toward every person. Whatever the situation, he will serve you; and whatever his hand finds to do, he will do it. He gives his fruit in his season, as often as God or man needs his works.

LW, 14, pp. 298, 300-301

Empty Before the Lord

When I called, Thou didst answer me, O God of my righteousness. In tribulation Thou didst make room for me. Psalm 4:1

The best way to lift the mind up to God is to acknowledge and ponder past blessings. The setting forth of past blessings is the guarantee of future ones, and gifts received in the past offer the confidence of receiving them. On the contrary, the total sinking of the mind away from God down to hell consists in forgetting or failing to take note of goods received.

Therefore, one must begin with thanksgiving and confession. The psalmist takes note of the good things received in prosperity and the good things received in adversity. He reflects upon both in brief words but in very broad thoughts.

See how true and godly is this confession, in which he arrogates nothing of merit to himself. He does not say, "Since I did much or earned much in deed or with the mouth or some other member of mine." He lays claim to no righteousness, he boasts of no merit, he displays no worth, but he praises the pure and exclusive grace and free kindness of God. He finds nothing within himself on the basis of which God should answer him. He only prays and keeps everything else quiet. Such a person "appears empty before the Lord" in the best way, because he is empty for himself but full for God.

LW, 10, pp. 45-46

The Shadow of Thy Wings

Hide me in the shadow of thy wings. Psalm 17:8b

The shadow of Thy wings in a mystical sense is faith in Christ, which in this life is mysterious and shadowy. But the wings of Christ are His hands stretched out on a cross. For just as the body of Christ on the cross produces a shadow, so it casts a spiritual shadow on the soul, namely faith in His cross, under which every saint is protected.

Second, the shadow of the wings is the protection and watch of the holy angels or of contemplative men, who are the wings of God, for in them He soars and dwells in affectionate and encaptured minds.

Third, the shadow of the wings is the learning of the Scriptures, in which there is rest for those who devote themselves to this learning. Thus the bride says in Song of Solomon 2:3: "I sat down under his shadow, whom I desired."

LW, 10, p. 111

Hear

The Lord is my Shepherd, I shall not want. Psalm 23:1

In this passage you hear that you lost sheep cannot find your way to the Shepherd yourself but can only roam around in the wilderness. If Christ, your Shepherd, did not seek you and bring you back, you would simply have to fall prey to the wolf.

But now He comes, seeks, and finds you. He takes you into His flock, that is, into Christendom, through the Word and the Sacrament. He gives His life for you, keeps you always on the right path, so that you may not fall into error. You hear nothing at all about your powers, good works, and merits—unless you would say that it is strength, good works, and merit when you run around in the wilderness and are defenseless and lost.

No, Christ alone is active here, merits things, and manifests His power. He seeks, carries, and directs you. He earns life for you through His death. He alone is strong and keeps you from perishing, from being snatched out of His hand (John 10:38).

And for all of this you can do nothing at all but only lend your ears, hear, and with thanksgiving receive the inexpressible treasure. Learn to know well the voice of your Shepherd, follow Him, and avoid the voice of the stranger.

LW, 12, pp. 154-157

My Instruction

I will instruct you and teach you the way you should go; I will counsel you with My eye upon you. Psalm 32:8

This is where I want you to be. You ask that I deliver you. Then do not be uneasy about it, do not teach Me, and do not teach yourself; surrender yourself to Me. I am competent to be your Master. I will lead you in a way that is pleasing to Me. You think it is wrong if things do not go as you feel they should. But your thinking harms you and hinders Me. Things must go, not according to your understanding but above your understanding. Submerge yourself in a lack of understanding, and I will give you My understanding. Lack of understanding is real understanding; not knowing where you are going is really knowing where you are going. My understanding makes you without understanding.

Thus Abraham went out from his homeland and did not know where he was going. He yielded to My knowledge and abandoned his own knowledge. By the right way he reached the right goal.

Behold, that is the way of the cross. You cannot find it, but I must lead you like a blind man. Therefore not you, not a man, not a creature, but I, through My Spirit and the Word, will teach you the way you must go. You must not follow the work which you choose, not the suffering which you devise, but that which comes to you against your choice, thoughts, and desires. There I call; there you must be a pupil; there it is the time; there your Master has come; there you must not be a horse or an irrational animal. If you follow Me and forsake yourself, behold, then "I will counsel you with My eye upon you."

LW, 14, pp. 147, 152

Christ's Lips

Thou art fair beyond the sons of men. Grace is overflowing upon Thy lips. Psalm 45:2

The poet has diligently read the prophecies and promises regarding Christ. He has seen that Christ's lips are the sweetest and loveliest lips, which attract the hearts of all the weak.

He does not call them simply "gracious" lips, but lips "overflowing with grace," in order to point out that Christ is superabundant in His lips. From His mouth, as from some overflowing fountain, the richest promises and teachings stem, and with these He strengthens and comforts souls.

Grace is on the lips of this King. Not only that, it overflows, so that you may understand how abundantly this fountain of grace flows and gushes forth. It is as though the psalmist said: "Our King has wisdom such as no man has, namely the sweetest and loveliest wisdom. He helps the penitent, comforts the afflicted, recalls the despairing, raises up the fallen and humiliated, justifies sinners, gives life to the dying."

Christ Himself says in Isaiah 50:4: "The Lord has given Me the tongue of those who are taught, that I may know how to sustain with a word him that is weary."

So mark this well. The tongue of Christ is not the kind that terrifies or hurts, except when He speaks to the proud and obstinate. This psalm speaks of the work which He exercises toward His own. Here nothing is heard but the voice of comfort for the lowly, the voice of joy, and the voice of the bridegroom.

LW, 12, pp. 210-213

His Bride and Queen

The queen stands at Thy right hand in golden clothing. Psalm 45:9b

The remission of sins and the whole treasure of divine mercy cannot be more excellently painted or described than that the church should be called the bride of Christ. It follows from this picture that the bride has everything that is Christ's. What does Christ have? Eternal righteousness, wisdom, power, truth, life, joy, grace. This is a most beautiful transformation, that the church, miserable in the eyes of men, should be so richly adorned in the eyes of God.

Therefore these are great and incomparable words, to hear that Jesus Christ is the Bridegroom and the church is the bride. In fact, they are heavenly and infinite words. They cannot be grasped by the heart of any man nor ever be learned completely. To anyone who brags that he knows these things you should say that he has merely heard some echo of this teaching but is ignorant of the matter itself.

I am saying this as an encouragement to you to ponder these words of the Holy Spirit. He speaks them for our comfort, in order that we may learn to extend them richly. No one can hear too much about this or grasp Christ too firmly. Grasp as much as you can, and you will still see that you are lacking something and that you cannot trust as much in the Bridegroom as He requires and we need. Satan, sin, flesh, blood, and our reason are still present. They oppose your grasping Him. And yet if you grasp Him, whether little or much, you have the Bridegroom, and through Him life and salvation.

LW, 12, pp. 259, 261-263

God of the Promise

Have mercy on me, O God, according to Thy steadfast love; according to Thy abundant mercy blot out my transgressions. Psalm 51:1

David is talking with the God of his fathers—the God who promised. The people of Israel did not have a God who was viewed "absolutely." Human weakness cannot help being crushed by the majesty of the absolute God, as Scripture reminds us over and over. Let no one, therefore, interpret David as speaking with the absolute God.

He is speaking with God as He is dressed and clothed in His Word and promises, so that from the name "God" we cannot exclude Christ, whom God promised to Adam and the other patriarchs. We must take hold of this God, not naked but clothed and revealed in His Word. Otherwise certain despair will crush us.

This distinction must always be made between the Prophets who speak with God and the pagans. Pagans speak with God outside His Word and promises, according to the thoughts of their own hearts. But the Prophets speak with God as He is clothed and revealed in His promises and Word. This God, clothed in such a kind appearance and dressed in His promises—this God we can grasp and look at with joy and trust. The absolute God, on the other hand, is like an iron wall, against which we cannot bump without destroying ourselves. Therefore Satan is busy day and night, making us run to the naked God so that we forget His promises and blessings shown in Christ and think about God and the judgment of God.

But David speaks with the God of his father, with the God whose promises he knows and whose mercy and grace he has felt. He could depend on God's promises as he prayed because the promises include Christ.

LW, 12, pp. 312—313

The Sacrifice of Righteousness

Then wilt Thou accept the sacrifice of righteousness, offerings, and burnt offerings. Then they will offer bulls over Thy altar. Psalm 51:19

You can understand all the sacrifices correctly—those that were done according to the Law and spiritual sacrifices. Both are sacrifices of righteousness, because their whole power is in the goodness of God and in divine blessing. When men trust in mercy this way, then if an ox is offered, it pleases God and is a sacrifice of righteousness. If there is no ox, then the "ox of our lips," as Hosea calls it (Hos. 14:2) pleases Him. This is the way I interpret all sacrifices. They are called sacrifices of righteousness, not because they justify but because they are done by those who are justified or righteous. Because the people are righteous and know that they please God by grace alone, not by some worthiness or merits of their own, whatever they do according to the Word of God is truly called either a sacrifice or a work of righteousness.

In the psalm David sets forth a double standard. The first is what he calls "a contrite heart." This is the first and most powerful sacrifice. After you have thus acknowledged God to be the Justifier of sinners, if you sing to God even one song of thanks, you add another sacrifice, namely a sacrifice of thanksgiving for the gift you have received. This sacrifice is not merit but a confession and testimony of the grace which your God has bestowed upon you out of sheer mercy.

Thus the saints and the righteous in the Old Testament brought burnt offerings with the purpose not of being justified through them, but of testifying that they had received mercy and comfort.

LW, 12, pp. 408-409

Pour Out Your Heart

Trust in Him at all times, O people; pour out your heart before Him; God is a Refuge for us. Psalm 62:8

Hope in God, for He will not let you down. Others laugh, comfort, and make promises, but do not pin your hopes on them. Do not depend on them, for both their strength and their courage are uncertain. Strength fades, courage fails; God remains firm. In times of adversity and in times of prosperity, therefore, you may depend on God.

If you are lacking something, well, here is good advice: "Pour out your heart before Him." Voice your complaint freely, and do not conceal anything from Him. Regardless of what it is, just throw it in a pile before Him, as you open your heart completely to a good friend. He wants to hear it, and He wants to give you His aid and counsel. Do not be bashful before Him, and do not think that what you ask is too big or too much. Come right out with it, even if all you have is bags full of need. Out with everything; God is greater and more able and more willing than all our transgressions. Do not dribble your requests before Him; God is not a man whom you can overburden with your begging and asking. The more you ask, the happier He is to hear you. Only pour it all out, do not dribble or drip it. For He will not drip or dribble either, for He will flood you with a veritable deluge.

"God is a Refuge for us," our Hiding Place, He and no one else.

LW, 14, pp. 237-238

Christ's Enemies

The Lord said to my Lord: "Sit at My right hand, till I make Thy enemies Thy footstool." Psalm 110:1

Observe this for your comfort: here these enemies are never called our enemies, or those of Christendom, but enemies of the Lord Christ. "Thy enemies," he says, although they really attack Christendom and Christians must suffer and be plagued by them, as it actually happens. For Christ, who sits above at the right hand of the Father, cannot be attacked. They cannot hurt one hair of His head, much less drag Him down from His throne. Still they are properly called His enemies, not ours.

For the world and the devil do not attack and plague us because of secular matters or because we have merited or caused it. The only reason for it is that we believe this Lord and confess His Word. For this reason He must deal with them as enemies who attack His person. Everything that happens to the individual Christian, whether it comes from the devil or from the world, such as the terrors of sin, anxiety and grief of the heart, torture, or death, He regards as though it happened to Him. He also says through the prophet Zechariah (Zech. 2:8): "He who touches you touches the apple of My eye." And in Matthew 25:40 we read: "As you did it to one of the least of these My brethren, you did it to Me."

Though we may feel the terrors of sin, anxiety and grief of heart, torture, and death, we are to remember that these are not our enemies but the enemies of our Lord, who is of our flesh and blood. We are to view Him as the Enemy of our enemies. In this comfort we are to direct them away from ourselves to Christ: "Do you not know? God has already judged you and pronounced you the footstool of Christ."

LW, 13, pp. 227, 262

Remembering Christ

He has made a remembrance of His wonderful works. The Lord is gracious and merciful. Psalm 111:4

Now, if you are afraid to go to the Sacrament and your conscience frightens you, as if you were unworthy, put this verse into your heart and on your lips. Then you must hear and feel how sincerely Christ calls and invites you. He is here and is waiting for you with hands and heart wide open, for you to take and receive grace and mercy. He does not want you to flee and shy away from Him but to flee to Him and with full confidence go to Him. Here He is called nothing but this: the gracious and merciful Lord. Do not give Him a different name in your heart or make Him anything else in your conscience. You would do Him an injustice and a great wrong, and yourself the greatest harm.

Whoever is inclined to put pictures on the altar ought to have the Lord's Supper of Christ painted, with these two verses written around it in golden letters: "The gracious and merciful Lord has instituted a remembrance of His wonderful works." Then they would stand before our eyes for our heart to contemplate them, and even our eyes, in reading, would have to thank and praise God.

Thus this verse expresses not merely the fruit and benefit of the Sacrament—that it is a gracious and merciful institution in which one should seek and find grace and mercy—but it also exalts the remembrance of Christ.

LW, 13, pp. 371, 373-375

Light Rises for the Upright

Light rises in the darkness for the upright; the Lord is gracious, merciful, and righteous. Psalm 112:4

Light, joy and pleasure, all things, are received by the upright man from Him who is gracious, merciful, and righteous toward him. It is based on his conviction that his heart is right with Him who is good, gracious, and merciful. Then he has no misgivings but is confident.

The hypocrites and the wicked also call God gracious, merciful, and righteous. But they do not understand it. They read and sing and preach about it, but there is a big difference. It is one thing to preach, sing, and say that God is all these things. It is quite another to feel the gracious, merciful, and righteous God in the heart. The pious and upright have this not only on their tongue but also in their heart. When the tongue and the heart agree, then it is well. But if this lies in the mouth alone, and the heart is a hundred thousand miles away, then it is futile. Christians feel and experience it in their heart that those matters do not happen accidentally or come from man. They feel it in their heart, are sure about it, and do not doubt.

Now, he who feels this in his heart will be satisfied. The light rises for him in the darkness. When the darkness is past, he also becomes rich and rises high, even if he is poor and oppressed. For he has Him who is gracious and merciful. Now, if he has Him who is the Fountain and Source of all things, what could he lack?

LW, 13, pp. 391, 405

Study the Word

Praise the Lord, all you heathen! Extol Him, all you peoples! For His steadfast love and faithfulness toward us prevails forever. Hallelujah! Psalm 117

This is a short, easy psalm, doubtless made this way so that everyone might pay more attention to it and remember better what is said. No one can complain about the length or content, much less about the sharpness, difficulty, or profundity of the words. Here we find only short, precise, clear, and ordinary words, which everyone can understand if he will only pay attention and think about them.

All God's words demand this. We must not skim over them and imagine we have thoroughly understood them as the frivolous, smug, and bored souls do. When they hear some word of God once, they consider it old hat and cast about for something new. This is a dangerous disease, a clever and malicious trick of the devil. Thus he makes people bold, smug, forward, and ready for every kind of error and schism.

All this, as I see it, is the result of reading and listening to God's Word carelessly instead of concentrating on it with fear, humility, and diligence.

I have often felt this particular devil and temptation myself. But I dare not say in my heart: "The Lord's Prayer is worn out; you know the Ten Commandments; you can recite the Creed." I study them daily and remain a pupil of the Catechism. I feel, too, that this helps me a lot, and I am convinced by experience that God's Word can never be entirely mastered, but that Ps. 147 speaks truly; "His understanding is beyond measure" (v. 5), or Ecclesiasticus: "Who drinks of me shall thirst even more after me" (24:29).

LW, 14, pp. 3, 7-8

He Is Good

O give thanks to the Lord, for He is good; His steadfast love endures forever! Psalm 118:1

You must not read the words "good" and "His steadfast love" with dull indifference. Nor dare you skim over them as some read the Psalter. No, you must bear in mind that these are vibrant, significant, and meaningful words. They express and emphasize one theme: God is good, but not as a human being is good. From the very bottom of His heart He is inclined to help and do good continually. He is not given to anger or inclined to punish except where necessary and where persistent, impenitent, and stubborn wickedness compels and drives Him to it. A human being would not delay punishment and restrain anger as God does; he would punish a hundred thousand times sooner and harder than God does.

This verse also serves to comfort us in all our misfortunes. We are such softies, such sapless sufferers. A pain in the leg can cause us to fill heaven and earth with our howls and wails, our grumbling and cursing. But the good God permits such small evils to befall us merely in order to arouse us snorers from our deep sleep and to make us recognize, on the other hand, the incomparable and innumerable benefits we still have.

We also are to look at our misfortunes in no other way than that with them God gives us a light by which we may see and understand His goodness and kindness in countless other ways. Then we conclude that such small misfortunes are barely a drop of water on a big fire or a little spark in the ocean.

LW, 14, pp. 47, 49-50

Distress

Out of my distress I called on the Lord; the Lord answered me and set me free. Psalm 118:5

Let everyone know most assuredly and not doubt that God does not send him this distress to destroy him. He wants to drive him to pray, to implore, to fight, to exercise his faith. In this way he learns another aspect of God's person and accustoms himself to do battle even with the devil and with sin, and by the grace of God to be victorious. Without this experience we could never learn the meaning of faith, the Word, Spirit, grace, sin, death, or the devil. Were there only peace and no trials, we would never learn to know God Himself. In short, we could never be or remain true Christians. Trouble and distress constrain us and keep us within Christendom.

We read: "I called upon the Lord." You must learn to call. Do not sit by yourself or lie on a couch, hanging and shaking your head. Do not destroy yourself with your own thoughts by worrying. Do not strive and struggle to free yourself. Mourn and pray as this verse teaches. Likewise Psalm 141:2 says: "Let my prayer be counted as incense before Thee, and the lifting up of my hands as an evening sacrifice!" Here you learn that praying, reciting your troubles, and lifting up your hands are sacrifices most pleasing to God. It is His desire and will that you lay your troubles before Him. He does not want you to multiply your troubles by burdening and torturing yourself. He wants you to be too weak to bear and overcome such troubles; He wants you to grow strong in Him. By His strength He is glorified in you. Out of such experiences men become real Christians.

LW, 14, pp. 58, 60-61

The Holy Christian Church

This is the gate of the Lord; the righteous shall enter through it. Psalm 118:20

Hypocrites, scoundrels, and sinners entered the gate of that temple; but only the righteous and the saints enter this gate of the Lord in order to serve Him. For no one can enter the Christian congregation or be a member of Christendom unless he is a believer, that is, righteous and holy, as the article of the Creed says: "I believe in the Holy Christian Church."

Therefore I hope that by this time almost everybody knows that whoever prides himself on being a Christian must also take pride in being holy and righteous. Since Christendom is holy, a Christian must also be righteous and holy, or he is not a Christian. All Scripture calls Christians holy and righteous, as does this verse. This is not boastfulness. It is a necessary confession and an article of faith.

We must realize that in our persons as children of Adam we are damned sinners, without any righteousness or holiness of our own. However, since we are baptized and believe in Christ, we are holy and righteous in Christ and with Christ. He has taken our sin from us and has graced, clothed, and adorned us with His holiness. Therefore anyone who hesitates to boast and confess that he is holy and righteous is actually saying: "I am not baptized. I am not a Christian. I do not believe that Christ died for me. I do not believe a word of what God has declared of Christ and all Scripture testifies."

But we are assured that the whole Christian Church is holy, not by itself or by its own work but in Christ and through Christ's holiness, as St. Paul says: "He has cleansed her by the washing of water with the Word" (Eph. 5:26).

LW, 14, pp. 91-93

45

God's Righteousness

For Thy name's sake, O Lord, preserve my life! In Thy righteousness bring me out of trouble! . . . For I am Thy servant. Psalm 143:11-12

I live in grace. Therefore my whole life serves Thee, not myself, for I seek not myself but Thee and Thine. Those who live in their own righteousness cannot do this. They serve themselves and look for their own welfare in all things.

Now someone might say to me: "Can't you ever do anything but speak only about the righteousness, wisdom, and strength of God rather than of man, always expounding Scripture from the standpoint of God's righteousness and grace, always harping on the same string and singing the same old song?"

I answer: Let each one look to himself. As for me, I confess: Whenever I found less in the Scriptures than Christ, I was never satisfied; but whenever I found more than Christ, I never became poorer. Therefore it seems to me to be true that God the Holy Spirit does not know and does not want to know anything besides Jesus Christ, as He says of Him (John 16:13-14): "He will glorify Me; He will not speak of Himself, but He will take of Mine and declare it to you."

Christ is God's grace, mercy, righteousness, truth, wisdom, power, comfort, and salvation, given to us by God without any merit on our part. Christ, I say, not as some express it in blind words, "causally," that He grants righteousness and remains absent Himself, for that would be dead. Yes, it is not given at all unless Christ Himself is present, just as the radiance of the sun and the heat of the fire are not present if there is no sun and no fire.

LW, 14, pp. 203-204

My Victory

The Lord God is my Strength and my Song. He has become my Salvation. Isaiah 12:2

Here we have proclaimed the blessings of God that make us safe from our enemies. For the Strength is my strength, the victorious power through which I have my enemies under my feet and shall trample the serpent underfoot. The Song is my psalm and the subject matter of my psalm and song. I have no one to sing and chant about but Christ, in whom alone I have everything. Him alone I proclaim, in Him alone I glory, for He has become my Salvation, that is, my victory. For thus the word "salvation" is often used in the Scriptures for "victory," as in 1 Sam. 14:45.

Our Victory is Christ, and when we boast of Christ, we shall win. Satan and the ungodly hear the Word of God not willingly but unwillingly. Yet this Word consoles and lifts up the godly who are alarmed either in the hour of death or in want and misfortune. By means of studying the Word of God is Satan thrown out, not by means of plans made by the flesh.

Therefore, have confidence in the Holy One of Israel, that is, Christ, who is great, unconquered, yes, all things for you. Although we are earthen vessels (2 Cor. 4:7), we tread Satan underfoot in Christ. He who is in us is greater than he who is in the world, as 1 John 4:4 says.

LW, 16, pp. 129-131

Hide a Little While

Come, My people, enter your chambers. Hide yourselves for a little while. Isaiah 26:20

God admonished the people here as in Psalm 4:4, when He said: "Be angry, but sin not; commune with your own hearts on your beds and be silent." Do not complain and cry out in times of persecution, but enter your chambers, keep quiet, do not be angry and impetuous. But pray to the Lord in secret and make your complaint to Him, as Peter says of Christ: "When He was reviled, He did not revile in return" (1 Peter 2:23), but kept silent, that is, He entered into His chamber.

"Hide yourselves for a little while," that is: "Wait a little and endure, because My wrath and your persecution are sudden and last only a moment. Therefore, see to it that you bear it for a little while. Do not erupt, because none of our troubles in the world are everlasting but only transitory." These are the riches of divine consolation that support us in every kind of trouble.

Soon after these words He says: "For behold, the Lord is coming" (Isaiah 26:21). The Lord will punish His persecutors and will not permit much blood of His saints to be shed.

LW, 16, pp. 209-210

Wait, Wait, Wait

In returning and rest you shall be saved. In quietness and in trust shall be your strength. Isaiah 30:15

Translate it thus: "If you will sit down and be quiet, you shall be saved. Do not lose heart and do not lose your temper. Wait till the storm blows over and keep still." Now that is a marvelous victory, to conquer by sitting and waiting! Meanwhile the flesh runs and toils and looks for help.

But trust in God, be patient, and commit everything to Him. In a wonderful way you will see God as your protector. This passage is an outstanding, golden, and magnificent promise: "In sitting quietly you shall be saved." Be calm, wait, wait, commit your cause to God, He will make it succeed. Look for Him a little at a time; wait, wait. But since this waiting seems long to the flesh and appears like death, the flesh always wavers. But keep faith. Patience will overcome wickedness.

The prophet further impresses this when he says: "Blessed are all those who wait for Him" (Isaiah 30:18), that is to say, they who wait for God are the holy, the good, and the godly. These wait for God, even when He takes His time. Therefore the blessed are saved. Everything would turn out all right, if you could only wait. Therefore, in all trouble let us wait for God, and we shall be blessed.

LW, 16, pp. 258-261

The Cross for Weak Hands

Strengthen the weak hands. Isaiah 35:3

This is a wonderful comfort that is to be understood not in a physical but in an internal sense, because it shines under the appearance of the cross. The members of the church are exposed to all, to Satan and to the craftiness and power of the world and the flesh. Therefore the prophet comforts them with exceedingly great consolations.

Strengthen the weak hands, he commands. Give medicine to those hands that are so weary, so that you become strong again. For Satan has two ways of fighting. He would gladly cast the faithful down suddenly from their joy and faith and into fear and despair. Secondly, he cunningly strives by long lasting torments and by the unremitting pressure of the torments to tire them out. These attacks are extremely powerful, and against Satan's continuous attack we must set our continuous divine help. The devil is a spirit at leisure and thinks of nothing but to take us by storm. We ought not have slack and idle hands over against his deceptions.

We ought to strengthen ourselves with these words and say, "Though all devils were rolled into one, my God is still greater." The afflicted must be comforted with such spiritual consolations of the Word, not with fleshly comfort which does nothing for troubled consciences. With spiritual comfort and with the living Word of God the afflicted are made strong.

LW, 16, pp. 300-301

Christ Does Not Weary

Have you not known? Have you not heard? The Lord is the everlasting God, the Creator of the ends of the earth. He does not faint or grow weary. Isaiah 40:28

This is a wonderful proclamation concerning God—He does not faint or grow weary. This seems mad to reason. But the prophet is depicting God in terms of our senses, as if he were saying: "We get tired and are worn out by Satan's plotting and cunning tricks. But you have a God who does not get tired. He will set you free from the incessant stratagems of Satan. Satan and the world are our relentless enemies. They keep after us until at last they exhaust us."

Therefore God consoles those who labor and are wearied: "I will not become weary. I have always been active, I am fresh and new. I can help you." Remembering this a certain nun by the name of Mechtild kept repelling the onslaughts of Satan with one word: "I am a Christian."

So I, too, must say: "I am dead, but Christ lives; I am a sinner, but Christ is righteous. I believe in Jesus Christ and was baptized in His name." Thus when we are fatigued, let us run to the fresh and untiring Christ and not remain with ourselves.

LW, 17, pp. 29-30

His Understanding

His understanding is unsearchable. Isaiah 40:28c

The Hebrew word means understanding—the power and acuteness of wisdom. It is as if He were saying: "Let them be as wise and acute as they wish. I will be more than a match for them and be wise. Just stay with Me. Look at Me as you would at a mirror. In you there is death, sin, despair, destruction. In Me there is life, righteousness, consolation, and deliverance. Since My Word is everlasting, cling to it. Do not dwell on your own thoughts."

It is natural for us who are beset by sins to struggle in our own thoughts. "But you must not give place to them. Instead, drive them out by the Word. Do not pursue your own thoughts in tribulation, because then you will fall into a sea of temptation. Rather, keep thinking of Me, because there is no search of the understanding directed against you. I will be more than a match for them. They first have to overpower Me."

LW, 17, p. 30

Faint

He gives power to the faint. Isaiah 40:29

Here you must understand what it means to be faint and impotent, in opposition to carnal reason which wants to be strong and most powerful. Reason willingly hears one thing—that God gives strength, but it does not want to be worn out and nothing. So all the self-righteous willingly receive strength from God, but they do not want to be faint, as if God would not give strength to the weary. What need is there for the secure to receive strength?

But God gives strength to the weary, the oppressed, and the troubled. The emphasis lies on the word "faint," but we look for the stress on the word "power." It is as if God were saying: "You must be weary and emptied, so that there is no way out for you. Then I will give you strength. First you must become nothing, then consolation and strength will come."

Therefore let us learn to console ourselves when we are afflicted and say, "What I do not have and what I cannot do, that Christ has and can do."

LW, 17, p. 31

Soft-Spoken Christ

He will not cry or lift up His voice, or make it heard in the street. Isaiah 42:2

The prophet says that Christ Himself will not be noisy in the streets nor make Himself heard in the open. How does this jibe? The noise is of two kinds: the noise of wrath and that of love. He did indeed cry in the preaching proceeding from love, but not in a noisy way, as the self-righteous and other sects are noisy. In opposition to their harshest clamor the prophet depicts the office of Christ as being gentle and mild. This is to cry without being noisy, that is, teach gently without rage.

In other partisan groups and judgments and lawsuits there is nothing but accusation and shouting on the part of those who suffer wrong on both sides. Even the judge shouts when he passes sentence. Thus the self-righteous are most turbulent. Because all of them are by nature sad and stern, all of them are ready to pass judgment. They measure everything by the standard of their own life and most severely condemn everything else.

True righteousness, however, has compassion, while the false has condemnation. Here in Christ you see the gentlest and most agreeable appearance. This is what it means for a Christian not to raise his voice, that is, in an uproar, but rather in grace.

LW, 17, p. 64

Forsaken for a Moment

God said: For a brief moment I forsook you. Isaiah 54:7

Who can believe this, that every one of our tribulations is momentary and that God's wrath is a point in time? Nobody can believe this; in our feeling every tribulation seems eternal, although in the sight of God it is momentary. Our feelings, our heart and flesh, do not see the end, and therefore they do not believe that it is for a moment. When the wrath of God presses down on us, that point does not seem to be mathematical but eternal.

The highest remedy is to leave the appearance behind and to turn from the obvious to what is not obvious. Therefore He says here: "If only you would cling to Me and keep away from the obvious, which is only a point!" Then He continues: "With everlasting love I will have compassion on you." This is a most excellent comparison. The moment of tribulation and wrath is a small one, but the mercy is everlasting and perpetual.

Yes, learn how to make this globe. The forsakenness is the center, but the mercy is the endless orb. It is not a physical globe, but it pertains to faith and is perceived by the Word. Thus let us take care to be certain in the Word. Then in all outward afflictions we will know that they are a point and that the mercy of God is the endless circumference of the globe.

LW, 17, pp. 238-239

Anointed to Bring Good Tidings

The Spirit of the Lord God is upon Me, because the Lord has anointed Me to bring good tidings to the afflicted. Isaiah 61:1

It is Christ who is defined here as the One to whom the office of the Word has been committed. Be content with Him, the God incarnate. Then you will remain in peace and safety, and you will know God. Cast off speculations about divine glory; stay with Christ crucified, whom Paul and others preach. But those who immerse themselves in their own speculations about the divine, for example, why God spares so many Turks and condemns so many, they are plunged into confusion or despair because of such speculations. Since Christ and His office are here set forth, we must be content with that description.

It is because of His humanity and His incarnation that Christ becomes sweet to us, and through Him God becomes sweet to us. Let us therefore begin to ascend step by step from Christ's crying in His swaddling clothes up to His Passion. Then we shall easily know God. I am saying this so that you do not begin to contemplate God from the top, but start with the weak elements. We should busy ourselves completely with treating, knowing, and considering this man. Then you will know that He is the Way, the Truth, and the Life (John 14:6). So He set forth His weakness that we may approach Him with confidence.

LW, 17, pp. 329-331

Thanksgiving

. . . that they may be called oaks of righteousness, the planting of the Lord, that He may be glorified. Isaiah 61:3c

It is as if God said: "I will dress my Christians up as a paradise of righteousnesses, that they may be called oaks of righteousness, the planting of the Lord. They shall grow for Me in spite of the world's disapproval." Here the prophet describes a garden that is planted by God and continues to grow. All the trees of this garden are called righteous. In the world there are also very large trees like the cedars, but they are trees of unrighteousness and iniquity. But in this garden they will be righteous, planted by God. Thus it follows that a Christian does not just come into being, but he is planted and produced by the work of God, and Christ is the gardener. For through the Word one is uprooted from the world and transplanted into this garden and watered. In this way the prophet comforts himself and sets before himself Christianity as a most beautiful garden.

And then he states the reason—"that He may be glorified." This is our work, to praise and give thanks to God. It is as if he said: "In this garden there will be nothing, no ceremonies of the Law and no sacrifices, except a single fruit from the trees—glorification, praise, and thanksgiving." The letters will stand on all the leaves. What lovely trees they are, having "thanksgiving" imprinted on them!

LW, 17, p. 336

All His Benefits

I will recount the steadfast love of the Lord, the praises of the Lord, according to all that the Lord has granted us. Isaiah 63:7

Now the prophet sings a song and gathers the praises into a poem. In all of Scripture it is customary for all the saints and prophets to console themselves in times of trial by recalling past benefits.

The prophet is not speaking of just one benefit. He wants to embrace all of them. This is not a mean art but the art of the Holy Spirit. Reason cannot sing about the Lord's blessings. It is the work of the Spirit alone to understand the mercies of the Lord. It is the wise man who begins to praise and give thanks. Reason of itself cannot do this. It only observes the threats and terrors of God and the ungodliness of the world, and then it begins to murmur and blaspheme. Why? Because the flesh cannot enumerate the blessings; it lists only the bad things and not the good things. Reason sees the world as extremely ungodly, and therefore it murmurs. The Spirit sees nothing but God's benefits in the world and therefore begins to sing. This calls for wisdom.

LW, 17, pp. 355-356

He Is Answering

Before they call I will answer. Isaiah 65:24

This is a very lovely promise: "I will answer before they call." This promise is extremely necessary for strengthening our hearts and inciting them to pray. In the presence of God our prayers are regarded in such a way that they are answered before we call. The prayer of the righteous man is answered before it is finished. Before the prayer begins to formulate, while the petitioner is still speaking in general, it is answered as in Psalm 21:2: "Thou hast given him his heart's desire."

So Bernard says to his brothers: "Do not despise prayers, and know that as soon as you will have raised your voices, they are written in heaven, and it will come to pass and it will be given you. If it is not given, then it is not good for you, and God will give you something in its place that is better and more useful." This statement of Bernard comes from the Holy Spirit.

Thus if I pray, I am anticipating a great thing in my prayer. And our prayer pleases God; He requires it and delights in it. He promises, commands, and shapes it. God cannot get enough of the prayers of the godly. Therefore the prayer of the godly is likened to the most attractive odor which one cannot smell enough. Then He says: "I will hear."

LW, 17, pp. 392-393

Readiness to Forgive

Guard the doors of your mouth from her who lies in your bosom. Micah 7:5

Here the prophet does not want suspicion and hatred to exist between spouses. He wants the utmost love and good will which cannot exist without mutual trust. And yet he wants a limit to this trust, because it can happen that it is mistaken. For she is a human being. Although she fears God and pays heed to His Word, nevertheless, because she has Satan, the enemy, lying in wait everywhere and because human nature is weak, she can fall and disappoint your hope somewhere.

When you foresee this with your mind, you will be readier to forgive, and you will be less distressed if anything happens contrary to what you had hoped. Thus love will remain, and harmony will not be disturbed. For nothing has happened that was not anticipated, and love is readiest to forgive. This is indeed a rare gift, but because you are a Christian, remember that this ought to be your attitude.

And so with others, the Christian hates no one, and yet he trusts no one. If others show him some kindness, he considers this an advantage and delights in it, nevertheless in such a way that if the kindness should cease or some adversity should occur, he would not be provoked or begin to hate the other person. For those who are taught by the Holy Scriptures realize what is in man, and for this reason they place complete trust in God and not in a man; yet they love all equally and show kindness to all, even to their enemies.

This, then, is solid friendship and the most steadfast love. It has its source, not in our judgment but in the Holy Spirit, who urges our minds to follow the Word.

LW, 2, pp. 299-302

Christ's Words

He opened His mouth and taught them and spoke. Blessed are the
spiritually poor, for theirs is the kingdom of heaven. Matthew 5:2-3

This is a fine, sweet, and friendly beginning for Christ's instruction and preaching. He does not come like Moses or a teacher of the Law, with demands, threats, and terrors, but in a very friendly way, with enticements, allurements, and pleasant promises. In fact, if it were not for this report which has preserved for us the first dear words that the Lord Christ preached, curiosity would drive and impel everyone to run all the way to Jerusalem just to hear one word of it. And everyone would proudly boast that he had heard or read the very word that the Lord Christ had preached. That is exactly how it would really be if we had none of this in written form, even though there might be a great deal written by others. Everyone would say: "Yes, I hear what St. Paul and His other apostles have taught, but I would much rather hear what He Himself spoke and preached."

But now since it is so common that everyone has it written in a book and can read it every day, no one thinks of it as anything special or precious. Yes, we grow sated and neglect it, as if it had been spoken by some shoemaker rather than the High Majesty of heaven. Therefore it is in punishment for our ingratitude and neglect that we get so little out of it and never feel nor taste what a treasure, power, and might there is in the words of Christ. But whoever has the grace to recognize it as the Word of God rather than the word of man, will also think of it more highly and dearly and will never grow sick and tired of it.

LW, 21, pp. 7, 10

Spiritually Poor

Blessed are the spiritually poor. Matthew 5:3a

The doctrine and life of the whole world are founded only upon their having enough. Such a doctrine can only make people greedy, so that everyone is interested in nothing but amassing plenty and in having a good time, without need or trouble. And everyone concludes: "If that man is blessed who succeeds and has plenty, I must see to it that I do not fall behind."

Therefore Christ preaches a totally new sermon here for the Christians. Something is necessary other than possession of enough on earth. But you say: "What? Must all Christians, then, be poor? Dare none of them have money, property, popularity, power, and the like? What are the rich to do? Must they surrender all their property and honor, or buy the kingdom of heaven from the poor?"

No. It does not say that whoever wants to have the kingdom of heaven must buy it from the poor. The little word "spiritually" is added. Nothing is accomplished when someone is physically poor and has no money or goods. The command is to be "spiritually poor." He wants to discuss only the spiritual—how to live before God, above and beyond the external.

There is the example of David. He was an outstanding king, and he really had his wallet and treasury full of money, his barns full of grain. In spite of all this he had to be a poor beggar spiritually, as he sings of himself (Ps. 39:12): "I am poor, and a guest in the land." This is truly a heart that does not tie itself to property and riches.

LW, 21, pp. 10-13

Mourning

Blessed are those who mourn, for they shall be comforted. Matthew 5:4

Mourning and sorrow are not a rare plant among Christians, in spite of outward appearances. Daily, whenever they look at the world, they must see and feel in their heart so much wickedness, arrogance, contempt, and blasphemy of God and His Word, so much sorrow and sadness, which the devil causes in both the spiritual and the secular realm. Therefore they cannot have many joyful thoughts, and their spiritual joy is very weak. If they were to look at this continually and did not turn their eyes away from time to time, they could not be happy for a moment.

Simply begin to be a Christian, and you will soon find out what it means to mourn and be sorrowful. If you can do nothing else, then get married, settle down, and make a living in faith. Love the Word of God, and do what is required of you in your station. Then you will experience, both from your neighbors and in your own household, that things will not go as you might wish. You will be hindered and hemmed in on every side, so that you will suffer enough and see enough to make your heart sad. But especially the dear preachers must learn this well and be disciplined daily with all sorts of envy, hatred, scorn, ridicule, ingratitude, contempt, and blasphemy. In addition, they have to stew inside, so that their heart and soul is pierced through and continually tormented.

Those who mourn this way are entitled to have fun and to take it wherever they can so that they do not completely collapse for sorrow. Christ also adds these words and promises this consolation so that they do not despair in their sorrow nor let the joy of their heart be taken away and extinguished altogether, but mix this mourning with comfort and refreshment.

LW, 21, pp. 20-21

Works that Shine

Let your light so shine before men that they may see your good works and give glory to your Father who is in heaven. Matthew 5:16

What He calls "good works" here is the exercise, expression, and confession of the teaching about Christ and faith, and the suffering for its sake. He is talking about works by which we "shine." This shining is the real job of believing or teaching, by which we also help others to believe. These are the works whose necessary conse-quence must be "that the heavenly Father is honored and praised."

Matthew is not writing about ordinary works that people should do for one another out of love about which he talks in Matthew 25:35 ff. Rather he is thinking principally about the distinctly Christian work of teaching correctly, of stressing faith, and of showing how to strengthen and preserve it. This is how we testify that we really are Christians. The other works are not such a reliable criterion, since even sham Christians can put on the adornment of big, beautiful works of love.

Thus the most reliable index to the true Christian is this: if from the way he praises and preaches Christ the people learn that they are nothing and Christ is everything. It is the kind of work that cannot remain hidden. It has to shine and let itself be seen publicly. That is always why it alone is persecuted, for the world can tolerate other works. This also entitles it to be called a work through which our Father is recognized and praised.

These are the works that should be first and foremost. They should be followed by those pertaining to our relations with our neighbor in what are called "works of love," which shine, too, but only insofar as they are ignited and sustained by faith.

LW, 21, pp. 64-66

Forgiving Others

If you forgive men their trespasses, your heavenly Father also will forgive you; but if you do not forgive men their trespasses neither will your Father forgive your trespasses. Matthew 6:14-15

This is a remarkable addition, but a very precious one. Someone may wonder why He should append this addition to "Forgive us our debts." He could just as well have appended some such item to one of the other petitions. He could have said: "Give us our daily bread, as we give it to our children."

By putting the petition this way, connecting the forgiveness of sin with our forgiving, He makes mutual love a Christian obligation. The continual forgiveness of the neighbor is the primary and foremost duty of Christians, second only to faith and the reception of forgiveness.

Christ attached this addition to the prayer to establish the closest possible bonds between us and to preserve His Christendom in the unity of the Spirit (Eph. 4:3), both in faith and in love. We must not let any sin or fault divide us or rob us of our faith and of everything else. It is inevitable that there be friction among us every day in all our social and business contacts. Things are said that you do not like to hear and things are done that you cannot stand. This gives rise to anger and discord. We still have our flesh and blood about us, behaving in its own way and easily letting slip an evil word or an angry gesture or action, which is an affront to love.

Therefore there must be continual forgiveness among Christians, and we continually need forgiveness from God, always clinging to the prayer: "Forgive us, as we forgive."

LW, 21, pp. 148-149, 154-155

Do So for Others

Whatever you wish that men would do to you, do so to them; for this is the Law and the Prophets. Matthew 7:12

With these words Christ concludes the teaching He has been giving in the Sermon on the Mount. He wraps it all up in a little package where it can all be found. Thus everyone can put it in his bosom and keep it.

It is as if He were saying: "Would you like to know what I have been preaching, and what Moses and all the Prophets teach you? I shall tell it to you so briefly and put it in such a way that you dare not complain about its being too long or too hard to remember." This is the kind of sermon that can be expanded or contracted. From it all teaching and preaching go forth and are broadcast, and here they come back together. How could it be put more succinctly and clearly than in these words?

The trouble is that the world and our old Adam refuse to let us ponder what He says and measure our lives against the standard of this teaching. We let it go in one ear and out the other. If we always measured our lives and actions against this standard, we would not be so coarse and heedless in what we do, but we would always have enough to do. We could become our own teachers, teaching ourselves what we ought to do.

LW, 21, p. 235

The Magnificat

My soul magnifies God, the Lord. Luke 1:46

These words of the tender mother of Christ express the strong ardor and exuberant joy with which all her mind and life are inwardly exalted in the Spirit. It is as if she said: "My life and all my senses float in the love and praise of God and in lofty pleasures, so that I am no longer mistress of myself. I am exalted, more than I exalt myself, to praise the Lord."

This is the experience of all those who are saturated with the divine sweetness and Spirit. They cannot find words to utter what they feel. For to praise the Lord with gladness is not a work of man; it is rather a joyful suffering and the work of God alone. It cannot be taught in words but must be learned in one's own experience. Even as David says in Psalm 34:8: "Oh, taste and see that the Lord is sweet; blessed is the man that trusts in Him." He puts tasting before seeing, because this sweetness cannot be known unless one has experienced and felt it for himself. And no one can attain to such experience unless he trusts in God with his whole heart when he is in the depths and in sore straits.

We must also give heed to Mary's last word, which is "God." She does not say, "My soul magnifies itself" or "exalts me." She does not desire herself to be esteemed. She magnifies God alone and gives all glory to Him. She leaves herself out and ascribes everything to God alone, from whom she received it. She had no thought but this: if any other maiden had got such good things from God, she would be just as glad and would not grudge them to her. Indeed, she regarded herself alone as unworthy of such an honor and all others as worthy of it.

LW, 21, p. 302-303, 308

Rejoice in God

My spirit rejoices in God, my Savior. Luke 1:47

Truly, Mary sets things in their proper order when she calls God her Lord before calling Him her Savior, and when she calls Him her Savior before recounting His works. Thereby she teaches us to love and praise God for Himself alone, and in the right order, and not selfishly to seek anything at His hands. This is done when one praises God because He is good, regards only His bare goodness, and finds his joy and pleasure in that alone. That is a lofty, pure, and tender mode of loving and praising God and well become this Virgin's high and tender spirit.

But the impure and perverted lovers, who are nothing else than parasites and who seek their own advantage in God, neither love nor praise His bare goodness. They have an eye to themselves and consider only how good God is to them—that is, how deeply He makes them feel His goodness and how many good things He does to them. So long as this feeling continues, they esteem Him highly, are filled with joy, and sing His praises. But just as soon as He hides His face and withdraws the rays of His goodness, leaving them bare and in misery, their love and praise are at an end. They are unable to love and praise the bare, unfelt goodness that is hidden in God. By this they prove that their spirit did not rejoice in God, their Savior, and that they had no true love and praise for His bare goodness. They delighted in their salvation much more than in their Savior, in the gift more than in the Giver, in the creature rather than in the Creator.

LW, 21, p. 309

God's Regard

He has regarded the low estate of His handmaiden. For behold, henceforth all generations will call me blessed. Luke 1:48

Mary confesses that the foremost work God did for her was that He regarded her, which is indeed the greatest of His works, on which all the rest depend and from which they all derive. For where it comes to pass that God turns His face toward one to regard him, there is nothing but grace and salvation, and all gifts and works must follow. Thus we read in Genesis 4:4, 5 that He had regard for Abel and his offering, but for Cain and his offering He had no regard. Here is the origin of the many prayers in the Psalter—that God would lift up His countenance upon us, that He would not hide His countenance from us, that He would make His face shine upon us and the like. And that Mary herself regards this as the chief thing, she indicates by saying: "Behold, since He has regarded me, all generations will call me blessed."

Note that she does not say men will speak all manner of good of her, praise her virtues, exalt her virginity or her humility, or sing of what she has done. But for this one thing alone, that God regarded her, men will call her blessed. That is to give all the glory to God as completely as it can be done.

LW, 21, pp. 312, 321

Resurrection

I will raise him up at the Last Day. John 6:54b

You must not judge by external appearances. You must be guided by the Word which promises and gives you everlasting life. Then you truly have eternal life.

Even though your senses tell you otherwise, this does not matter. This does not mean that you have forfeited life, for sickness, death, perils, and sin which assail you will not devour or finish you. They will have to leave you in peace. They do not weaken or kill Christ. When these all have passed and have left you constant in your faith, then you will see what you have believed.

But you retort: "The fact remains that I must die."

This makes no difference! Go ahead and die in God's name. You are still assured of eternal life; it will surely be yours. To die, to be buried, to have people tread on your grave, to be consumed by worms—all this will not matter to you. It is certain that Christ will raise you up again. For here you have His promise: "I will raise you up."

Therefore your eyes will behold what your faith so confidently relied on.

LW, 23, p. 131

Hear Him

If any man's will is to do His will, he shall know whether the teaching is from God. John 7:17

Now this is the will of the Father, that we be intent on hearing what the Man Christ has to say, that we listen to His Word. You must not quibble at His Word, find fault with it, and dispute it. Just hear it.

Then the Holy Spirit will come and prepare your heart, that you may sincerely believe the preaching of the divine Word, even give up your life for it, and say: "This is God's Word and the pure truth." But if you insist that you be heard, that your reason interpret Christ's Word; if you presume to play the master of the Word, to propound other doctrines; if you probe it, measure it, and twist the words to read as you want them to, brood over them, hesitate, doubt, and then judge them according to your reason—that is not hearing the Word or being its pupil. Then you are setting yourself up as its schoolmaster. In that way you will never discover the meaning of Christ's Word or of His heavenly Father's will.

Simply hear what the Son of God says. Hear His word, and adhere to it. It is written: "Hear Him!" To hear, to hear—that is the command, and thus we truly conform to God's will. He has promised to give the Holy Spirit to him who hears the Son, to enlighten and inflame him to understand that it is God's Word. God will make a man out of him after His own heart. This He will surely do.

LW, 23, pp. 229-230

Consolation

Let not your hearts be troubled. John 14:1a

Christ knows that if we want to remain His own and adhere to Baptism, the Sacrament, and the Gospel, the devil will inevitably be our enemy, incessantly pressing us with all his might and contending for our body and soul. Even if God wards him off and prevents him from killing you in one day, he will nevertheless craftily and cunningly persist in trying at least to rob you of your courage and security. He will try to fill you with disquietude and sadness, and subsequently to bring you into other dangers and distress. Christ here wants to exhort and console us, that we may be reconciled to our lot and not be too alarmed or let the devil subdue us so easily and make us despair and lose courage.

From these and similar words of Christ we should learn to know the Lord Christ aright, to develop a more cordial and comforting confidence in Him. We are to learn to pay more regard to His Word than to anything else which may confront our eyes, ears, and other senses.

For if I am a Christian and hold to Him, I always know that He is talking to me. Here and elsewhere I learn that all His words are intended to comfort me. Yes, all He says, does, and thinks are nothing but friendly and consoling words and works. To this end He promises to send His disciples and the Christians the Holy Spirit, whom He calls the Comforter.

LW, 24, pp. 9, 12-13

Finding God

Believe in God, believe also in Me. John 14:1b

Christ wants to say here: "You have heard that you must trust in God. But I want to show you where you will truly find Him, lest your thoughts create an idol bearing the name of God. If you want to believe in God, then believe in Me. If you want to apply your faith and your confidence properly, that it may not be amiss or false, then direct it toward Me, for in Me the entire Godhead dwells perfectly."

Later Christ declares (John 14:6, 9): "I am the Way, the Truth, and the Life. He who has seen Me has seen the Father. He who hears Me hears the Father." Therefore, if you want to be sure to meet God, take hold of Him in Me and through Me.

Repeatedly in the Gospels Christ declares that He was sent by the Father. He says and does nothing of His own accord but states that it is the Father's order and command to all the world to believe Christ as God Himself. Thus no one dare adopt another person or another means to apprehend God than this one Christ. He assures us that if we rely on Him, we will not encounter an idol, as the others do who resort to other ways to deal with God.

It is certain that he who bypasses the Person of Christ never finds the true God. Since God is fully in Christ, where He places Himself for us, no effort to deal with God without and apart from Christ on the strength of human thoughts and devotion will be successful.

Whoever would travel the right road and not go astray with his faith, let him begin where God says and where He wants to be found, in this man—Jesus Christ.

LW, 24, pp. 17, 23

Comforter

I will pray the Father, and He will give you another Comforter, to be with you forever. John 14:16

Here we must note in what a friendly and comforting manner Christ speaks to all poor, saddened hearts and fearful, timid consciences. He shows us how we may truly recognize the Holy Spirit and feel His comfort. We must learn to know and believe in the Holy Spirit as Christ describes Him. His is not a Spirit of anger and terror but a Spirit of grace and consolation. We are to know that the entire Deity reflects sheer comfort. The Father wants to comfort, for it is He who grants the Holy Spirit. The Son likewise, for He prays for this. And the Holy Spirit Himself is to be the Comforter. Here, therefore, there is no wrath, threat, or terror for Christians; there is only a friendly smile and sweet comfort in heaven and on earth.

But we forget. The devil is too powerful among us, the world is too strong, and we see so many obstacles and temptations before us that we forget and cannot comprehend the comfort God sends into our hearts. We feel only that which hurts us. It is so strong that it fills man's whole being and erases these words from his mind.

Therefore Christians should rise above all fear and sadness and hear Christ: "I know this very well, and for this very reason I am telling you about it in advance. You should not be guided by such feelings or believe your own thoughts; you should believe My Word. For I will ask the Father, and He will surely give you the Holy Spirit to comfort you. Then you can rest assured that I love you, the Father loves you, and the Holy Spirit, who is sent to you, loves you."

LW, 24, pp. 103, 110-111, 114

Peace

Peace I leave with you; My peace I give to you; not as the world gives do I give to you. John 14:27

It is a very comforting and pleasing bequest that Christ leaves His disciples. It does not consist of cities and castles or of silver and gold. It is peace, the greatest treasure in heaven and on earth. He does not want His disciples to be fearful and mournful. He wants them to have true, beautiful, and longed-for peace of heart.

"For so far as I am concerned," Christ says, "you shall have nothing but sheer peace and joy. All My sermons to you and all My associations with you have let you see and realize that I love you with all My heart and do for you everything that is good, and that My Father is most graciously disposed toward you. That is the best I can leave to you and give you, for peace of heart is the greatest peace. Hence the expression, 'Joy of heart exceeds all other joy, sadness of heart surpasses all other woe.' I am leaving you this precious and great treasure: a good, fine, and peaceful heart toward God and Me. For I am leaving you the Father's and My love and friendship. You have seen and heard nothing but kind and friendly words and works from Me. And these are not Mine; they are the Father's. Thus you possess everything you could desire from Me, even though I am leaving you and you see Me no more."

LW, 24, pp. 177-178

The Vinedresser

I am the true Vine, and My Father is the Vinedresser. Every branch of Mine that bears no fruit He takes away, and every branch that does bear fruit He prunes, that it may bear more fruit. John 15:1-2

This is a very comforting picture and an excellent, delightful personification. Here Christ does not present a useless, unfruitful tree to our view. No, He presents the precious vine, which bears much fruit and produces the sweetest and most delicious juice, even though it does not delight the eye. He interprets all the suffering which both He and His Christians are to experience as nothing else than the diligent work and care of a vinedresser.

This requires the art of believing and being sure that whatever hurts and distresses us does not happen to hurt or harm us but is for our good and profit. We must compare this to the work of the vinedresser who hoes and cultivates his vine. If the vine could talk and saw the vinedresser chopping about its roots with a mattock and cutting wood from its branches with a pruning hook, it would say: "What are you doing? Now I must wither and decay. You are removing the soil from my roots and belaboring my branches with those iron teeth."

But God is not a tyrant. He is a pious Vinedresser who tends and works His vineyard with all faithfulness and diligence and surely does not intend to ruin it. He does not let His vineyard stand there to be torn to pieces by dogs and wild sows; He tends it and watches over it. He is concerned that it bear well and produce good wine. Therefore He must hoe and prune so as not to chop and cut too deeply into the stem and the roots, take off too many branches, or trim off all the foliage. Let us be unafraid. Let us not be terrified by the prongs and teeth of the devil and the world; for God will not let them go beyond what serves our best interests.

LW, 24, pp. 193-194, 199

Abide in Me

If you abide in Me, and My words abide in you. John 15:7a

Note how highly this Man extols the Christian life. Someone may not have understood and would like to ask: "But how, my dear Man, does one remain in Christ? How am I a branch in this Vine, or how do I remain a branch?"

Christ answers: "Just pay attention to My Word. Everything depends on whether My Word remains in you, that is, whether you believe and confess the article taught in the children's (Apostles') Creed: 'I believe in Jesus Christ, our Lord, who was crucified for me, who died, rose again, and is seated at the right hand of the Father,' and whatever pertains to it. If you remain faithful to this and are ready to stake all on it, to forsake all rather than accept a different doctrine or works, if you thus remain in the Word, then I remain in you and you in Me. Then our roots are intertwined; then we are joined, so that My words and your heart have become one. Then you will not ask further how I abide in you or you in Me, for you will see this in yonder life. Now, however, you can grasp and comprehend it in no other way than that you have My Word, that you are washed in My blood by faith, and that you are anointed and sealed with My Spirit. Therefore your whole life and all your deeds are acceptable and nothing but good fruit."

LW, 24, pp. 238-239

The Christian Estate

Ask whatever you will, and it shall be done for you. John 15:7b

Open your mouth confidently, as a little child speaks to its father, who is pleased with everything it does if only it comes to him. The father is especially glad to comply with all the child's requests if it chats with him in a childlike manner when it asks him for something. Not only that, but he also provides for the child, and his one concern is to supply all the child's needs.

Hence Christians enjoy a great and glorious advantage if they remain pure and firm in the faith and guard against false doctrine and impure living. This is a splendid and comforting sermon on the estate of being a Christian.

Where is there a calling or walk of life on earth about which there are so many splendid promises as about this one? And these promises pertain to all who are called Christians and are baptized, whether monk or layman, master or servant, mistress or maid, young or old. This must indeed be an estate blessed and prized above all others, to which the divine promise is assured that whatever those in it ask of and desire from God shall surely be granted and shall be yea and amen before God. Besides, everything that is done in this estate shall be approved and praised by God. Should we not be willing to wander to the ends of the earth in search of such a promise? Now it is carried before our very door without any toil or cost on our part, for the benefit of all who will accept it.

LW, 24, pp. 238-240

Love One Another

This is My commandment, that you love one another as I have loved you. . . . You are My friends if you do what I command you. John 15:12, 14

It is surely kind and pleasing that Christ calls His disciples His friends. For He would like to encourage and rouse us to pay heed to His love, to consider how He made the Father our Friend and how He proved Himself our Friend above all friends. But all of us who are His friends must also live in friendship with one another.

Thus He gives this kind commandment. The Lord, who gave body and soul and did everything for us, does not demand payment of us for this, as though we had to do so for His sake. He asks that we do something in our own interest. From Him we have everything for nothing, and all that is required of us is that we help one another.

Christ says: "I ask you to love one another, to be loyally attached to one another, and to serve one another in a friendly way—all this in your own best interest. I am commanding you to do nothing more than to love one another as I have loved you. After all, it is only natural for you to do this, and it should be done spontaneously."

For it is natural—and everybody must admit this—that everyone would like to be shown love, fidelity, and help. Therefore we have been intermingled by God in order that we may live side by side and serve and help one another. God has no need whatever of such service and help, nor does He give this command for His sake. But we, of course, need it in our inmost hearts.

LW, 24, pp. 248, 251-253

Knowing God

All that I have heard from My Father I have made known to you. John 15:15

These are beautiful and comforting words. Christ says to us: "If you want to know the Father's will and thought in heaven, you have all the information right here, for I have told you everything." A Christian can arrive at this definite conclusion and say: "God be praised, I know everything that God wants and has at heart. Nothing that serves my salvation is concealed from me."

Christ is not saying that we are to have an answer to every question, but that we are to be informed about God's whole plan and counsel for us. If you want to be certain what God in heaven thinks of you, you must not seclude yourself, retire into some nook, and brood about it. Neither should you seek the answer in your works or in your contemplation. Banish all this from your heart. Give ear solely to the words of this Christ, for everything is revealed in Him.

And here He declares: "I was sent to you by My Father that I might shed My blood and die for you. As a token of this you have Baptism and the Sacrament, and I ask you to believe this. Here you have all that I know and have heard from the Father. The Father has no other plan and intention toward you than to save you if you have Christ and faith. From this you see how I love you, and what friendship, glory, joy, consolation, and assurance you have from Me. You cannot attain this anywhere else, either in heaven or on earth."

LW, 24, pp. 256-257

True Righteousness

When the Comforter comes, He will convince the world of sin and of righteousness and of judgment: . . . of righteousness, because I go to the Father, and you will see Me no more. John 16:8, 10

These words show exhaustively that Christ is not speaking here of outward, secular righteousness, which is important and necessary for this life. He is speaking here of a righteousness recognized by God, a righteousness far different from that acknowledged by the world. This righteousness He exalts far above all the works that can be done in this life and identifies it exclusively with Himself.

This is a peculiar righteousness. It is strange indeed that we are to be called righteous or to possess a righteousness which is really no work, no thought, in short, nothing whatever in us but is entirely outside us in Christ. Yet it becomes truly ours by reason of His grace and gift, and becomes our very own, as though we ourselves had achieved and earned it.

Reason, of course, cannot comprehend this way of speaking, which says that our righteousness is something which involves nothing active or passive on our part, yes, something in which I do not participate with my thoughts, perception, and senses; that nothing at all in me makes me pleasing to God and saves me; but that I leave myself and all human thoughts and ability out of account and cling to Christ, who sits up there at the right hand of God and whom I do not even see.

But in this verse I hear Christ say that my righteousness consists of His ascension into heaven. There my righteousness has been deposited, and there the devil will surely have to let it remain; for he will not make Christ a sinner or reprove or find fault with His righteousness.

LW, 24, pp. 336, 345-348

The Spirit of Truth

When the Spirit of truth comes, He will guide you into all the truth. John 16:13a

The Holy Spirit will teach the disciples and show them that everything Christ told them is the truth, for He is a Spirit who confirms the truth in one's heart and makes one sure of it.

The dear apostles surely found out, and their conduct toward their Lord Christ demonstrated adequately, how completely impossible—not only difficult—it is to retain faith in trials if one does not have the help of the Holy Spirit. In Christ's suffering and death they deserted Him ignominiously. They denied Him, and the faith in their hearts was practically extinguished by the thoughts inspired by the devil.

Thus true Christians always have discovered and still do that this faith, which should hold firmly to the articles concerning Christ and His kingdom, cannot be retained by human reason or power. The Holy Spirit Himself must accomplish this. It is a sure sign of the presence of the Holy Spirit and of His power when faith is preserved and is victorious in a real battle and trial.

All experience and the work itself show daily that in Christendom the Holy Spirit Himself must do everything that pertains to the real guidance of Christendom. For without Him we would not baptize or preach very long, nor would we retain the name of Christ. In one hour the devil would have dispossessed us of everything and would have destroyed it.

LW, 24, pp. 357, 359-360

85

The Speaker, the Word, and the Listener

Whatever the Holy Spirit hears He will speak. John 16:13c

Here it is relevant to state that Scripture calls our Lord Christ—according to His divine nature—a "Word" (John 1:1) which the Father speaks with and in Himself. Thus this Word has a true, divine nature from the Father. It is not a word spoken by the Father as a physical, natural word spoken by a human being is a voice or a breath that does not remain in him but comes out of him and remains outside him. No, this Word remains in the Father forever. Thus these are two distinct Persons: He who speaks and the Word that is spoken, that is, the Father and the Son.

Here, however, we find the third Person following these two, namely the One who hears both the Speaker and the Spoken Word. For there must also be a listener where a speaker and a word are found. But all this speaking, being spoken, and listening takes place within the divine nature and also remains there, where no creature is or can be. All three—Speaker, Word, and Listener—must be God Himself. All three must be coeternal and in a single undivided majesty. For there is no difference or inequality in the divine essence, neither a beginning nor an end. Therefore, one cannot say that the Listener is something outside God, or that there was a time when He began to be a Listener. But just as the Father is a Speaker from eternity, and just as the Son is spoken from eternity, so the Holy Spirit is the Listener from eternity.

LW, 24, pp. 362, 364-365

Magnifying God's Grace

Why not do evil that good may come?—as some people slanderously charge us with saying. Romans 3:8

The apostle is not speaking primarily against those who are open sinners. He is speaking against those who appear righteous in their own eyes and trust in their own works for salvation. He is trying to encourage these people to magnify the grace of God, which cannot be magnified unless sin which is forgiven through this grace is first acknowledged and magnified.

This is why the others, when they heard this, were offended and thought that the apostle is preaching that evil should be done, so that the glory of God might be magnified. For in this way do our iniquity and our lying "abound to His glory" (v. 7), when we, humbled through the confession of them, glorify God, who has forgiven such wickedness out of His overflowing grace. He would not be glorified in this way if we did not believe that we are in need of His grace but thought that we were sufficient of ourselves in His sight. Thus he is better off who acknowledges that he has many sins and no righteousness than he who like a Pharisee acknowledges that he has much righteousness and no sin. For the one glorifies the mercy of God, but the other his own righteousness.

LW, 25, pp. 27-28

Satan's Tricks

On the principle of works? No, but on the principle of faith. Romans 3:27

The devil, that master of a thousand tricks, lays traps for us with marvelous cleverness. He leads some astray by getting them involved in open sins. Others, who think themselves righteous, he brings to a stop, makes them lukewarm, as Rev. 3:14 ff. indicates. A third group he seduces into superstitions and ascetic sects, so that, for example, they do not at all grow cold but feverishly engage in works, setting themselves apart from the others, whom they despise in their pride and disdain. A fourth class of people he urges on with ridiculous labor to the point where they try to be completely pure and holy, without any taint of sin.

He senses the weakness of each individual and attacks him in this area. And because these four classes of people are so fervent for righteousness, it is not easy to persuade them to the contrary. Thus he begins by helping them to achieve their goal, so that they become overanxious to rid themselves of every evil desire. When they cannot accomplish this, he causes them to become sad, dejected, wavering, hopeless, and unsettled in their consciences.

Then it only remains for us to stay in our sins and to cry in hope of the mercy of God that He would deliver us from them. Just as the patient who is too anxious to recover can surely have a serious relapse, we must also be healed gradually and for a while put up with certain weaknesses. For it is sufficient that our sin displeases us, even though we do not get entirely rid of it. For Christ carries all sins, if only they are displeasing to us, and thus they are no longer ours but His, and His righteousness in turn is ours.

LW, 25, pp. 251, 254

Righteousness and Peace

Since we are justified by faith, we have peace with God through our Lord Jesus Christ. Romans 5:1

In this chapter the apostle speaks as one who is extremely happy and full of joy. In the entire Scripture there is scarcely another text like this chapter, scarcely one so expressive. For he describes the grace and mercy of God in the clearest possible manner, telling us what it is like and how great it is for us.

Note how he begins, placing spiritual peace with God only after righteousness has preceded it. For first he says, "since we are justified by faith," and then, "we have peace." But the perversity of men seeks peace before righteousness, and for this reason they do not find peace. Thus the apostle creates a very fine antithesis in these words, namely,

The righteous man has peace with God but affliction in the world, because he lives in the Spirit.

The unrighteous man has peace with the world but affliction and tribulation with God, because he lives in the flesh.

But as the spirit is eternal, so also will be the peace of the righteous man and the tribulation of the unrighteous.

And as the flesh is temporal, so will be the tribulation of the righteous and the peace of the unrighteous.

LW, 25, pp. 43, 285-286

Love from Faith

Now we are discharged from the Law, dead to that which held us captive, so that we serve not under the old written code but in the new life of the Spirit. Romans 7:6

But how are we "discharged from the Law?" Doubtless because through faith in Christ we satisfy the demands of the Law and through grace are freed and voluntarily perform the works of the Law. But he who does not have this faith is active in works unwillingly and almost in fear or in a desire for his own convenience. Therefore love is necessary, which seeks the things of God, love which is given to him who asks in faith and in the name of Jesus.

Even though we sin often and are not perfectly voluntary, yet we have made a beginning and are progressing, and we are righteous and free. But we must constantly beware that we not fall back under the Law. For who knows whether or not he is acting out of fear or a love for his own convenience even in a very subtle manner in his devotional life and his good works, looking for rest and a reward rather than the will of God?

Therefore we must always remain in faith and pray for love.

LW, 25, pp. 59-60

"Feet" for the Gospel

How beautiful are the feet of those who preach the Gospel of peace.
Romans 10:15

In the first place, they are called "beautiful" because of their purity, since they do not preach the Gospel for personal advangage or empty glory, but only out of obedience to God as well as for the salvation of the hearers.

In the second place, the term "beautiful" according to the Hebrew idiom has more the meaning of something desirable or hoped for, something favored or worthy of love and affection. Thus the meaning is that the preaching of the Gospel is something lovable and desirable for those who are under the Law.

But what is meant by the term "feet"? According to the first interpretation the term refers to the attitude and the devotion of those who preach, which must be free of all love of money and glory.

But according to the Hebrew, which is more accurate, the term "feet" can be taken in a literal sense, namely, that the coming of preachers of good things is something desirable for those who are tortured by sins and an evil conscience. And even more correctly the term can signify their very words themselves or the sound and the syllables, the pronunciation of the words of those who preach. For their voices are like feet or vehicles or wheels by which the Word is carried or rolled or it walks to the ears of the hearers. Hence the psalmist says: "Their voice goes out through all the earth" (Ps. 19:4). And again: "His Word runs swiftly" (Ps. 147:15). Whatever runs has feet: the Word runs, therefore the Word has feet, which are its pronunciations and its sounds. While the hearer sits quietly and receives the Word, the "feet" of the preacher run over him.

LW, 25, pp. 415-417

The Work of Prayer

Be constant in prayer. Romans 12:12

This is spoken in opposition to those who only read the Psalms without any heart. And we must be on our guard that the prayers in church in our day do not become more of a hindrance than a help. First, because we offend God more by reading them when our heart is not in it, as He says: "This people honors Me with their lips, etc." (Matt. 15:8; Mark 7:6; Is. 29:13). Second, because we are deceived and made secure by the appearance of these things, as if we had truly prayed properly. And thus we never become really attached to the desire for true prayer, but when we pray these things, we think that we have prayed and are in need of nothing more. This is a terrible danger.

This is the reason why he inserted the word "constant," a great watchword that must be noted and respected by all, and especially by clerics. For this word signifies that we must put real work into our praying. And it is not in vain. For as the ancient fathers have said: "There is no work like praying to God."

Therefore, when a man wants to enter the priesthood, he must first consider that he is entering a work which is harder than any other, namely the work of prayer. For this requires a subdued and broken mind and an elevated and victorious spirit.

LW, 25, p. 458

Bring Peace

He who thus serves Christ is acceptable to God and approved by men.
Romans 14:18

First one ought to be acceptable to God because of one's righteousness which is by faith. Then one ought to be approved by men because of one's peacefulness. For one ought to seek not one's own things but the neighbor's.

Hence it is common to say of those who are restless and who disturb others that they do not have peace, because they will not allow others to live their lives in peace, but they disturb them. These people the apostle calls restless, 1 Thess. 5:12-14: "Be at peace with those who are over you, rebuke the restless, encourage the fainthearted, help the weak, be patient with them all." Those who are restless and disturb the peace are not "approved by men" but are displeasing to men.

Thus the apostle would have us not only be at peace but also bring peace, be quiet and modest toward one another. For he then says: "Let us then pursue what makes for peace" (v. 19), that is, those things which do not disturb others but which edify and calm them. And what are these things? The answer is: Love teaches us what they are as the time and the place require. For they cannot be given to us in the particular.

LW, 25, p. 505

Joy and Peace

May the God of hope fill you with all joy and peace in believing, so that by the power of the Holy Spirit you may abound in hope. Romans 15:13

Joy is a trusting conscience, and peace, mutual concord. The apostle puts joy first and then peace, because joy makes a man peaceful and composed in himself. When he has become composed, it is easy for him to make peace with others. But he who is sad and disturbed is easily upset at others and of a stormy mind.

All these things take place "in believing," because our joy and peace do not consist in something material but are beyond material things, in hope. Otherwise the God of hope would not give them, for He gives good things which are hidden, joy in sadness and personal affliction, peace in the midst of tumult and outward persecution. Where faith is lacking, a person falls in sadness and persecution, because material things, in which he had placed his trust while they were available, fail him. But persecution causes hope to abound, as he said in chapter 5:4: "Trial produces hope."

And this is "by the power of the Holy Spirit." It is not because we trust in our own abilities that "trial produces hope." Then we would still be weak and powerless under persecutions. But "the Spirit helps us in our weakness," so that we cannot only hold out but be made perfect and triumphant.

LW, 25, p. 518

Christic in Me

I live; yet not I, but Christ lives in me. Galatians 2:20a, b

Paul shows how he is alive, and he states what Christian righteousness is. It is that righteousness by which Christ lives in us. Christ and my conscience must become one, so that nothing remains in my sight but Christ, crucified and risen. If I look only at myself, then I am done for. By paying attention to myself and considering what my condition is or should be, and what I am supposed to be doing, I lose sight of Christ.

This is an extremely common evil. In such conflicts of conscience we must form the habit of leaving ourselves behind as well as the Law and all our works, which force us to pay attention to ourselves. We must turn our eyes completely to that bronze serpent, Christ nailed to the cross (John 3:14). We must declare with assurance that He is our Righteousness and Life. For the Christ on whom our gaze is fixed, in whom we exist, and who also lives in us, is the Victor and the Lord over the Law, sin, death, and every evil. In Him a sure comfort has been set forth for us, and victory has been granted.

Therefore, because Christ clings and dwells in us most imtimately, we can say: "Christ is fixed and cemented to me and abides in me. The life that I now live He lives in me. Indeed, Christ Himself is the life that I now live."

LW, 26, pp. 166-167

"Me"

The Son of God loved me and gave Himself for me. Galatians 2:20c

Read these words "me" and "for me" with great emphasis. Accustom yourself to accepting this "me" with a sure faith and applying it to yourself. Do not doubt that you belong to the number of those who speak this "me."

It is as though Paul were saying: "The Law did not love me. It did not give itself for me. It accuses and frightens me. Now I have Another, who has freed me from the terrors of the Law, from sin, and from death. He is One who has transferred me into freedom, the righteousness of God, and eternal life. He is called the Son of God."

Therefore Christ is not Moses, not a taskmaster or a lawgiver. He is the Dispenser of grace, the Savior and the Pitier. In other words, He is nothing but sheer, infinite mercy, which gives and is given.

For Christ is the joy and sweetness to a trembling and troubled heart. He is the One "who loved ME and gave Himself for me."

Christ did not love only Peter and Paul, but the same grace belongs and comes to us. We are included in this "me." For just as we cannot deny that we are sinners, so we cannot deny that Christ died for our sins.

LW, 26, pp. 172, 177-179

Inner Assurance

Because you are sons, God has sent the Spirit of His Son into your hearts. Galatians 4:6

We must not doubt that the Holy Spirit dwells in us. We must be sure and acknowledge that we are a "temple of the Holy Spirit" (1 Cor. 6:19). For if someone experiences love toward the Word, and if he enjoys hearing, speaking, thinking, lecturing, and writing about Christ, he should know that this is not a work of human will or reason but a gift of the Holy Spirit.

Therefore we should believe that whatever we say, do, or think is pleasing to God, not on our account but on account of Christ. We are most certain that Christ is pleasing to God and that He is holy. To the extent that Christ is pleasing to God and that we cling to Him, we, too, are pleasing to God and holy. Although sin still clings to our flesh and we still fall every day, still grace is more abundant and more powerful than sin.

This inner assurance that we are in a state of grace and have the Holy Spirit is accompanied by the external signs I have mentioned: to enjoy hearing about Christ; to teach, give thanks, praise, and confess Him; to do one's duty according to one's calling; to help the needy brother and comfort the sorrowful. By these signs we are assured and confirmed that we are in a state of grace.

LW 26, pp. 374, 376, 378-379

Abba

. . . crying: Abba! Father! Galatians 4:6c

It is a very great comfort that the Spirit of Christ, sent by God into our hearts, cries: "Abba! Father!" He helps us in our weakness and intercedes for us with sighs too deep for words. Anyone who truly believed this would not fall away in any affliction. But many things hinder this faith. Our heart was born in sin. Further, we have the innate evil in us that we doubt the favor of God toward us. We cannot believe with certainty that we are pleasing to Him. Besides, "our adversary, the devil, prowls around, issuing terrible roars" (1 Peter 5:8). He roars: "You are a sinner. Therefore God is wrathful with you and will destroy you forever." We have nothing to strengthen and sustain us except the bare Word, which sets Christ forth as the Victor over sin, death, and every evil. But it is effort and labor to cling firmly to this in the midst of trial and conflict. We do not see Christ, and in the trial our heart does not feel His presence and help. Then a man feels the power of sin, the weakness of the flesh, and his doubt. He feels the fiery darts of the devil (Eph. 6:16).

Meanwhile, the Holy Spirit is helping us in our weakness and interceding for us. He merely utters the words of a cry and a sigh, which is "Oh, Father!" This is indeed a very short word, but it includes everything. It is as if one were to say: "Even though I am surrounded by anxieties and seem to be deserted and banished from Thy presence, nevertheless I am a child of God on account of Christ. I am beloved on account of the Beloved."

Therefore the term "Father," when spoken meaningfully in the heart, is an eloquence that Demosthenes, Cicero, and the most eloquent men cannot attain.

LW, 26, pp. 380-381, 385

An Heir

If a son, then an heir through Christ. Galatians 4:7b

It transcends all the capacity of the human mind when Paul says "heirs," not of some very wealthy and powerful king, but of Almighty God, the Creator of all. If someone could believe with a certain and constant faith, he could regard all the power and wealth of all the world as filth in comparison with his heavenly inheritance. For what is the whole world in comparison with God, whose heir and son he is?

He would desire to depart and to be with Christ. Nothing more delightful could happen to him than a premature death, for he would know that it is the end of all his evils and that through it he comes into his inheritance. A man who believed this completely would not go on living very long. He would soon be consumed by his overwhelming joy.

But the law in our members at war with the law of our mind (Rom. 7:23) does not permit faith to be perfect. We need the aid and comfort of the Holy Spirit. Paul himself exclaims (Rom. 7:24): "Wretched man that I am! Who will deliver me from this body of death?" He did not always have pleasant and happy thoughts about his future inheritance in heaven. Over and over he experienced sadness of spirit and fear.

From this it is evident how difficult a thing faith is. For a perfect faith would soon bring a perfect contempt and scorn for this present life. We would not attach our hearts so firmly to physical things that their presence would give us confidence and their removal would produce dejection and even despair. But we would do everything with complete love, humility, and patience.

LW, 26, pp. 392-393

Faith—Internal and External

In Christ Jesus neither circumcision nor uncircumcision is of any avail, but faith working through love. Galatians 5:6

Here Paul presents the Christian life—faith that is neither imaginary nor hypocritical but true and living. It is a faith that arouses and motivates good works through love. He says: "It is true that faith alone justifies, without works. But I am speaking about genuine faith. After it has justified, it will not go to sleep but it is active through love."

Thus he describes the whole Christian life. Inwardly it is faith toward God, and outwardly it is love or works toward one's neighbor. In this way a man is a Christian in a total sense: inwardly through faith in the sight of God, who does not need our works; outwardly in the sight of men, who do not derive any benefit from our faith but do derive benefit from works or from our love.

Earlier Paul has discussed the internal nature, power, and function of faith and has taught that it is righteousness or rather justification in the sight of God. Here he connects it with love and works; that is, he speaks of its external function. He says that faith is the impulse and motivation of good works or of love toward one's neighbor. Thus what makes a Christian is true faith toward God, which loves and helps one's neighbor.

LW, 27, pp. 30-31

Christ—Gift and Example

You were running well; who hindered you from obeying the truth? This persuasion is not from Him who called you. Galatians 5:7-8

This comfort applies to all who, in their affliction and temptation, develop a false idea of Christ. For Satan has a thousand tricks and turns the comfort of Christ upside down by setting against it the example of Christ. He says: "But your life does not correspond to Christ's either in word or in deed. You have done nothing good." When this happens, he who has been assailed should comfort himself this way: "Scripture presents Christ in two ways. First as a gift. If I take hold of Him this way, I shall lack nothing whatever. As great as He is, He has been made by God my wisdom, righteousness, sanctification, and redemption (1 Cor. 1:30). Even if I have committed many great sins, nevertheless, if I believe in Him, they are swallowed up by His righteousness.

"Secondly, Scripture presents Him as an example for us to imitate. But I will not let this Christ be presented to me as exemplar except at a time of rejoicing, when I am out of reach of temptations, so that I may have a mirror in which to contemplate how much I am still lacking, lest I become smug. But in a time of tribulation I will only see and hear Christ as a gift, as Him who died for my sins, who has bestowed His righteousness on me, and who accomplished and fulfilled what is lacking in my life."

LW, 27, pp. 31, 33-34

Love Your Neighbor

The whole Law is fulfilled in one word: You shall love your neighbor as yourself. Galatians 5:14

Love is the highest virtue. It is neither called forth by anything that someone deserves nor deterred by what is undeserving and ungrateful. And no creature toward which you should practice love is nobler than your neighbor—that is, any human being, especially one who needs your help.

He is not a devil, not a lion or a bear, not a stone or a log. He is a living creature very much like you. There is nothing living on earth that is more lovable or more necessary. He is naturally suited for a civilized and social existence. Thus nothing could be regarded as worthier of love in the whole universe than our neighbor.

But such is the amazing craft of the devil that he is able not only to remove this noble object of love from my mind but even to persuade my heart of the exactly opposite opinion. My heart regards the neighbor as worthy, not of love but of the bitterest hatred. The devil accomplishes this very easily, suggesting to me: "Look, this man suffers from such and such a fault. He has chided you. He has done you damage." Immediately this most lovable of objects becomes vile. My neighbor no longer seems to be someone who should be loved but an enemy deserving of bitter hatred.

In this way we are transformed from lovers into haters. All that is left to us of this commandment are the naked and meaningless letters and syllables: "You shall love your neighbor as yourself."

LW, 27, pp. 55, 58

Flesh and Spirit

The desires of the flesh are against the Spirit, and the desires of the Spirit are against the flesh; for these are opposed to each other, to prevent you from doing what you would. Galatians 5:17

I remember that Staupitz used to say: "More than a thousand times I have vowed to God that I would improve, but I have never performed what I have vowed. Hereafter I shall not make such vows, because I know perfectly well that I shall not live up to them. Unless God is gracious and merciful to me for the sake of Christ and grants me a blessed final hour, I shall not be able to stand before Him with all my vows and good works." This despair is not only truthful but is godly and holy. Whoever wants to be saved must make this confession with his mouth and with his heart.

The saints do not rely on their own righteousness. They gaze at Christ, their Propitiator. If there is any remnant of sin in the flesh, they know that this is not imputed to them but is pardoned. Meanwhile they battle by the Spirit against the flesh. This does not mean that they do not feel its desires at all; it means that they do not gratify them. Even though they feel the flesh raging and rebelling against the Spirit and feel themselves falling into sins and living in them, they do not become downcast. No, they fortify themselves with their faith.

Therefore let no one despair when he feels his flesh begin another battle against the Spirit, or if he does not succeed immediately in forcing his flesh to be subject to the Spirit. But let him be aroused and incited to seek forgiveness of sins through Christ and to embrace the righteousness of faith.

LW, 27, pp. 70, 72-74

His Word in the Heart

Let the Word of Christ dwell in you richly. Colossians 3:16

One must ponder this Word constantly, and always some new fire to arouse the heart will be found. Christians never read the same teaching enough. For the Gospel does not concern itself with knowledge; it concerns itself with feeling. But we slip every day. The flesh, sin, death, and the world assail us. Not for even one moment are we safe from spiritual adultery. This is how it is because sins surround us on all sides and weaken godly feelings. Besides, the world persecutes us.

Hence it is necessary to hear the Word of God constantly, to proclaim the death of Christ constantly, and to ponder constantly, in order that our feelings may be enlightened. Christ says (Matt. 7:13): "And lead us not into temptation, but deliver us . . ." For no one is safe for even one hour, but all are daily in a most precarious state. Now they stand, now they fall, and now an evil conscience. Therefore, Christians must live every day by the Word as the body lives by food. He who does not have the Word or ponder it soon becomes a sorry wretch. If I do not reflect on a verse of a psalm or a statement of the Gospel, my heart is completely full of sins. A return to the Word guards against sins. The heart should always be grinding. If the grain, namely, the Word of God, is good, the flour will be good, and the bread will be good.

LW, 16, pp. 30-31

Christ's Loving-Kindness

When the goodness and loving-kindness of God our Savior appeared.
Titus 3:4

This "goodness" is a sweetness of life, not only goodness but also kindness. A man is kind or sweet when he is friendly and well-disposed, easily approachable, not harsh, but pleasant and joyful. He makes an effort to have people enjoy being about him. They are glad to hear him speak. He is companionable, affable, and easy for everyone to get alone with. He is a brother to every man you can think of. This is a sweet manner. This text sets forth Christ as one who has such "goodness," the sweetness of golden virtue and of deity. This "goodness" is that most gracious treatment of us and attitude toward us in Christ. Whoever was with Him preferred His company to that of the Pharisees.

When he says "loving-kindness," Paul is speaking about Christ's activity, not human nature. Christ lived among us in the sweetest of ways, offended no one, and tolerated everyone. With this sweetness He did not serve Himself but sought to show love and the effects of love toward blind men by giving them sight. He was eager to serve men out of generosity and friendliness.

And now God is so disposed toward us in Christ. For it is Christ who treats us sweetly, who does everything to help us, who gives His gifts, who gives teachers to teach the brethren and to help and strengthen us in bearing evils, who is present at death to receive our souls—in short, who wants to love people.

LW, 29, pp. 78-79

105

Christ's Humanity

In these last days God has spoken to us by His Son, whom He appointed the Heir of all things, through whom He made the worlds also. Hebrews 1:2

The writer describes the same Christ as the Son of Man and the Son of God. For the words "He was appointed the Heir of all things" are properly applicable to Him because of His humanity. But the words "the worlds were made through Him" apply to Him because of His divinity.

One should also note that he mentions the humanity of Christ before he mentions His divinity, in order that he may establish the well-known rule that one learns to know God in faith. For the humanity is that holy ladder of ours, mentioned in Gen. 28:12, by which we ascend to the knowledge of God.

Therefore Christ says: "No one comes to the Father but by Me" (John 14:6). And again: "I am the Door" (John 10:7). He who wants to ascend advantageously to the love and knowledge of God should abandon the human metaphysical rules concerning knowledge of the divinity and apply himself first to the humanity of Christ. For it is exceedingly godless temerity that, where God has humiliated Himself in order to become recognizable, man seeks for himself another way by following the counsels of his own natural capacity. For Christ is the image of the invisible God, as it says in Col. 1:15.

LW, 29, pp. 110-111

Works Flow from Faith

How shall we escape if we neglect such a great salvation? Hebrews 2:3

In the Law there are very many works—they are all external—but in the Gospel there is only one work—it is internal—which is faith. Therefore the works of the Law bring about external righteousness; the works of faith bring about righteousness that is hidden in God.

Consequently, when the Jews asked in John 6:28: "What must we do, to be doing the works of God?" Christ draws them away from a large number of works and reduces the works to one. He says: "This is the work of God, that you believe in Him whom He has sent" (John 6:29). Therefore, the whole substance of the new law and its righteousness is that one and only faith in Christ.

Yet it is not so one-and-only and so sterile as human opinions are, for Christ lives; not only lives but works, and not only works but reigns. Therefore it is impossible for faith in Him to be idle. It is alive, and it itself works and triumphs, and in this way works flow forth spontaneously from faith.

For in this way our patience flows from the patience of Christ, and our humility from His, and the other good works in like manner, provided that we believe firmly that He has done all these things for us, not only for us but also before our eyes, that is, as St. Augustine is wont to say, not only as a sacrament but also as an example.

LW, 29, p. 123

A Pleasing Spectacle

Jesus, the Author of their salvation. Hebrews 2:10

God the Father made Christ to be the Sign and Idea in order that those who adhere to Him by faith might be transformed into the same image (2 Cor. 3:18) and thus be drawn away from the images of the world. Therefore Isaiah says: "The Lord will raise an Ensign for the nations, and will assemble the outcasts of Israel," and "The Root of Jesse which stands as an Ensign to the peoples; Him shall the nations seek" (Isaiah 11:12, 10).

This gathering together of the sons of God is similar to what happens when the government arranges a spectacle to which the citizens flock. They leave their work and their homes and fix their attention on it alone. Thus through the Gospel as through a spectacle exhibited to the whole world (cf. 2 Cor. 4:9) Christ attracts all men by the knowledge and contemplation of Himself and draws them away from the things to which they have clung in the world.

In this way Christ is the Cause and Leader of salvation, for He draws and leads His sons to glory through Him. One would commonly say that Christ is the Instrument and the Means by which God leads His sons. For God does not compel men to salvation by force and fear, but by this pleasing spectacle of His mercy and love He moves and draws through love all whom He will save.

LW, 29, pp. 131-132

Faith Through Hearing

As the Holy Spirit says: Today if you hear His voice, do not harden your hearts. Hebrews 3:7

One should note that this is the one, and the greatest, thing God requires of all men, that they hear His voice. Therefore Moses impresses so many times throughout Deuteronomy: "Hear, O Israel" and "If you hear the voice of the Lord your God." Indeed, nothing resounds in the prophets more frequently than "hear," "they did not hear," and "they were unwilling to hear." And rightly so, because without faith it is impossible for God to be with us (cf. Heb. 11:6), or to work, since He does everything through His Word alone. Thus no one is able to cooperate with Him unless he adheres to the Word.

But human nature recoils violently from this hearing. Therefore, those who rely on their own counsel and "do not wait for the counsel of the Lord" (cf. Ps. 106:13) harden their hearts to their own immeasurable harm and impede the work of God in themselves. For God works beyond strength, beyond perception, beyond intention, and beyond every thought.

From this one now understands who the people are who annoy, irritate, exasperate, and contradict, as Scripture rather frequently speaks of them, namely the people who do not believe the Word of God and are impatient of the work of God. They follow their master as long as they are aware of visible things to rely on. If these things fail, they fail too. Therefore faith in Christ is an exceedingly arduous thing. It is a removal from everything one experiences within and without to the things one experiences neither within nor without, namely to the invisible, most high, and incomprehensible God.

LW, 29, pp. 147-149

Illumined from Above

When God made a promise to Abraham, . . . He swore by Himself, saying, "Surely I will bless you and multiply you." Hebrews 6:13a

Chrysostom says: "By means of these words the apostle comforts with rewards by showing God's customary way of doing things. It is not His custom to fulfill His promises swiftly but to do so after a long time." Therefore he who wants to serve God must learn to know His will and His custom. For who can serve a master whom he does not know?

But to learn to know God as a dog learns to know its master or in the way the philosophers learned to know His power and His essence (Rom. 1:20) is not enough. One must learn to know what His will or what His plan is.

This He shows in His commandments, as Ps. 103:7 states: "He made known His ways to Moses and His will to the Children of Israel." But no one understands His commandments, either, unless he is illumined anew from above. "For who among men will be able to know the counsel of God, or who will be able to think what God's will is?" (Wisd. 9:13). Likewise (1 Cor. 2:11, 10): "The things of God no one knows but the Spirit of God. But God has revealed them to us through His Spirit."

And so we read in Ps. 119: "Teach me," "Instruct me," "Give me understanding." With all these words not only God's essence but especially His will is commended. Therefore those who presume to grasp Holy Scripture and the Law of God with their own intellect and to understand them by their own effort are exceedingly in error. For this is the source of heresies and godless dogmas, since they approach, not as receptive pupils but as bustling teachers.

LW, 29, pp. 185-186

Loving Others

Let us consider how to stir up another to love. Hebrews 10:24

The church of this time has been gathered from the diverse believers of the world. Very many who are weak, impotent, imperfect, and sinful have been intermingled. But human nature is constituted in such a way that it prefers to deal with those who are good and perfect to dealing with those who are imperfect and difficult. Because of this sin, those who are weaker cause those who are more perfect to be haughty, to despise, to judge, etc. On the other hand, those who are more perfect cause those who are weaker to envy and disparage. Therefore the apostles strove with all their might to counter this evil, lest schisms and heresies arise in the church.

These, of course, are prevented only by mutual love. Furthermore, the love that is shown to equals or betters is (as one sees everywhere) either no love at all, or it is not Christian, as Matt. 5:43-47 states: "You have heard that it was said to those of old: 'You shall love your friend and hate your enemy.' But I say to you: 'Love your enemies, do good to those who hate you, pray for those who persecute and slander you. For if you love only those who love you, what reward will you have? Do not even the tax collectors do this?' "

This, therefore, is the Christian love that is shown to those who are comtemptible and unworthy of love. This, in fact, is the kindness that is bestowed on those who are evil and ungrateful. For this is what Christ and God did for us; and we, too, are commanded to love as He did.

LW, 29, pp. 226-227

A Gift for Others

You say, I am rich, I have prospered, and I need nothing; not knowing that you are wretched, pitiable, poor, blind, and naked. Revelation 3:17

It is the worst kind of vice and the most demonic kind of pride for us to commend ourselves and pat ourselves on the back if we see or feel some special gift in ourselves. We do not thank God for it, but we become so proud and contemptuous of others and so preoccupied with it that we do not pay attention to whatever else we are doing, and imagine that we are in fine shape.

If it is true that your gift is greater than somebody else's, this is as it must be, because your office is different, higher, and greater. But when you go on to use your gift as a mirror in which to admire yourself, you spoil it completely and make this sublime ornament filthier than everybody else's faults. The richer your gifts, the more abominable the perversion if you make them an idol. Thus you replace God with yourself in your own heart. You become arrogant toward your neighbor and so completely blind in everything that you can no longer know or see God or your neighbor or even yourself.

God did not give you your gifts for you to tickle yourself with them, but for you to help your neighbor with them when he needs it, and thus by your strength to bear his weakness, by your piety and honor to cover up his sin and to conceal his shame, as God through Christ has done for you and still does every day.

LW, 21, pp. 216-218